THE NEGRO

IN CONTEMPORARY AMERICAN LITERATURE

By ELIZABETH LAY GREEN

*An Outline for
Individual and Group Study*

CHAPEL HILL   MCMXXVIII
THE UNIVERSITY OF NORTH CAROLINA PRESS

COPYRIGHT, 1928, BY
THE UNIVERSITY OF NORTH CAROLINA PRESS

PRINTED BY CHRISTIAN PRINTING COMPANY IN
THE UNITED STATES OF AMERICA AT DURHAM, N. C.

THIS BOOK WAS DIGITALLY PRINTED.

TABLE OF CONTENTS

FOREWORD 5

Part I. Poetry

I. EARLY CONTRIBUTIONS OF THE NEGRO.. 7
   Negro Spirituals, Folk Songs and Rhymes—The Beginnings
   of Negro Poetry—Paul Laurence Dunbar.

II. CONTEMPORARY POETRY.. 10
    A General Survey—Spokesmen for the Race—Modernists.

III. THREE LEADING POETS.. 14
     William Stanley Braithwaite—James Weldon Johnson—
     Claude McKay.

IV. TWO YOUNGER POETS... 18
    Countee Cullen—Langston Hughes

Part II. Drama

V. THE NEGRO'S CONTRIBUTION TO THE ART OF THE THEATRE.............. 22
   The Gift of Song and Dance—Negro Actors—Negro
   Playwrights.

VI. DRAMA FOR NEGRO ACTORS.. 26
    Negro Life: Material for White Dramatists—*Granny
    Maumee*—Ernest Culbertson's *Goat Alley.*

VII. THE NEGRO PLAYS OF EUGENE O'NEILL.. 29
     The Material of O'Neill's Plays—*The Emperor Jones*—
     All God's Chillun Got Wings.

VIII. PAUL GREEN—INTERPRETER OF THE SOUTHERN NEGRO................ 33
      Short Plays of Negro Life—*The No 'Count Boy*—
      In Abraham's Bosom.

Part III. Fiction

IX. THE "OLD TIMEY" NEGRO AND HIS FOLK-LORE................................. 38
    The Southern Plantation, A Romantic Legend—The Uncle
    Remus Tales of Joel Chandler Harris—Recent Negro Folk-
    Tales.

X. THE NEGRO BECOMES A CENTRAL CHARACTER.................................. 42
   A General Survey of Recent Fiction—Negroes with
   a Thesis—Three Realistic Novels by White Writers.

TABLE OF CONTENTS

XI. TWO SOUTHERN NOVELISTS 48
        Julia Peterkin—*Black April*—DuBose Heyward's *Porgy*.

XII. NEGRO WRITERS OF FICTION 51
        Jean Toomer—Eric Walrond—Negro Short Story Writers.

Part IV. Criticism

XIII. THE OLD AND THE NEW IN RACE RELATIONS 56
        Booker T. Washington—The Leadership of W. E. B. Du
        Bois—The Essays of Du Bois.

XIV. "THE NEW NEGRO" 60
        The Negro Newspaper—Two Negro Magazines—*The New
        Negro*.

SPECIAL REFERENCE BIBLIOGRAPHY 63

MAGAZINE DIRECTORY 69

A PARTIAL LIST OF LITERATURE BY AND ABOUT THE NEGRO SINCE 1900 76

PUBLISHERS' DIRECTORY 93

TERMS FOR THE COURSE 95

SCHEDULE OF MEETINGS 96

FOREWORD

The present interest in the Negro artist appears to be a sufficient reason for singling out for special study these recent books which treat of the colored man. Only by isolating this particular material from the body of American literature can we come to a deeper understanding and appreciation of the Negro's place in our national life. In preparing this outline I have become impressed with the fact that the phenomenon of artistic activity by and about the Negro is no fad, is no local color interest which in a few years will belong to the past, but rather is something native to the life of America, something vital and alive, part of our strength and tradition, and should be cherished as such. The study course outlined here has no sociological aim other than the sympathy coincident with any recognition of artistic attainment.

Only fourteen subjects have been outlined. In case any group or individual wishes to devote more time to the course, some of the writers may be taken up more intensively, and additional study may be made of individual books of some one writer. Perhaps the most desirable way to enlarge this study would be to give more intensive treatment to the subject matter of Chapters IX and X.

For use in group study a more or less uniform plan has been carried out in apportioning to three different students at each meeting three separate papers, no one paper encroaching upon the subject matter of the other two. In the references the particular paper to which each article pertains has been indicated in parentheses. Where a reference is numbered (1, 2, 3) it contains material on all three papers. In sending out the material for the course, the Extension Division cannot furnish to each group every one of the long list of books and articles. An unusually large number of such references are given in the hope that the local library will be found to contain some of the material which will be helpful.

The books listed in the Special Reference Bibliography are, with few exceptions, in print and readily available to the student. Appended to this study is a "Partial List of Literature by and about the Negro since 1900." In compiling this bibliography from all sorts of stray sources, many of them unreliable, I have been handicapped by the lack of adequate library facilities, and many errors have occurred which otherwise might have been avoided. In spite of this, I hope it will not be entirely useless.

E. L. G.

May, 1928
Chapel Hill, N. C.

PART I. POETRY

CHAPTER I

EARLY CONTRIBUTIONS OF THE NEGRO

IN music and poetry the Negro so far has found his most natural means of expression. In the novel and in drama, forms of art demanding a more objective view of their subject matter, the white writer has surpassed the Negro, even in the use of his own materials. But poetry, particularly shorter verse, offers a means of more subjective expression. The folk-songs, religious and secular, reveal the most valuable attributes of the Negro as artist—his imagination, extreme emotionalism, gift for melodious phrasing—to treat only of the words without music. In contrast to the primitive and spontaneous simplicity of this folk-poetry, we have the efforts of a small body of half-educated writers, some of them pure-blooded African slaves. Poorly equipped and unconscious of the worth of their African background, they imitated Americans who in turn were developing little which was not imitative of England. Their work is valuable chiefly for its sociological and historical interest. More gifted than these forerunners, and more original, was Paul Laurence Dunbar, who remains today the most widely read Negro writer. At the time of the "local color" school in fiction he created genre studies of Southern plantation life which accorded with the traditional conception of the Negro. His use of dialect verse is his distinctive contribution, but his poems in the conventional manner must not be overlooked. There is in his poetry scarcely a trace of racial self-consciousness or the spirit of revolt which marks the present generation of poets.

Subjects for Study

1. NEGRO SPIRITUALS, FOLK-SONGS, AND RHYMES

a. The emotional experience of the slave, his joys and sorrows.
   His master's encouragement of religious excitation.
b. Probable origin of the spirituals. Influence of the Bible (Old Testament characters and imagery and the figure of Jesus from the New Testament) and of old hymn books. The words adapted to the melodies.
c. Characteristics of the race reflected. Contrast the sorrow songs with some humorous work-songs. The Negro's opinion of his master.

d. The seculars, ballads, work-songs, nursery rhymes, dance rhymes, etc. Present-day folk-songs such as the Blues.
e. Summary of the value of this simple folk-poetry.

2. The Beginnings of Negro Poetry

a. Phillis Wheatley. Her life, education, and achievement. Note that she is one of the first women in America to publish work. Compare her with Anne Bradstreet. Note that the faults of her work, her stilted and imitative style, are to be found in the poetry of most of the writers of the time.
b. George Moses Horton. His life as a slave, work as a janitor at the University of North Carolina, proficiency in rhyming, efforts to buy his freedom with his verses. Quote from his work.
c. James Madison Bell, Charles L. Reason, Alberry A. Whitman, Frances Watkins Harper.
d. The general handicaps under which these Negroes worked.
e. Compare their protests against slavery with the abolitionist poetry of such white writers as Whittier.
f. Their greatest faults—imitative, stilted, conventionally religious.
g. Their contribution. (For selections see the White and Jackson anthology.)

3. Paul Laurence Dunbar

a. Ancestry, early life, education.
b. Early writing. Success of his readings from his own work. His personality.
c. Patronage of William Dean Howells, who encouraged his dialect verse in particular. Note the vogue of "local color" in the fiction of such writers as Howells, Mary E. Wilkins Freeman, Thomas Nelson Page, and in the poetry of Field and Riley. Discuss this influence upon Dunbar. Consider his stories and novels.
d. Estimate his non-dialect poems. Read "Compensation," "Life," "Ere Sleep Comes Down to Soothe the Weary Eyes." An example of his expression of race pride is "Ode to Ethiopia."
e. The dialect poems, their phrasing, interpretation of the Negro. Is the author influenced by the white man's conception of the humor and pathos of the black? Read "When Malindy Sings," "When de Co'n Pone's Hot."

(For selections see the White and Jackson and Johnson anthologies. Substitutions may be made from Dunbar's *Complete Poems*.)

REFERENCES

(Numerals refer to subjects)

Brawley: *The Negro in Literature and Art*. Duffield. (1, 2, 3)
Cullen: *Caroling Dusk*. Harper. (1)

Curtis-Burlin: *Negro Folk Songs*, Hampton Series. Schirmer. (1)
    Songs and Tales from the Dark Continent. Schirmer. (1)
DuBois: *The Gift of Black Folk*. Stratford. (1, 2, 3)
    The Souls of Black Folk. McClurg. (1)
Dunbar: *Complete Poems*. Dodd. (3)
Gaines: *The Southern Plantation*. Columbia Press. (3)
Handy: *Blues*. Boni. (1)
Harris: *Uncle Remus, His Songs and His Sayings*. Appleton. (3)
Johnson: *The Book of American Negro Poetry*. Harcourt. (1, 2, 3)
Johnson and Johnson: *The Book of American Negro Spirituals*. Viking. (1)
    The Second Book of American Negro Spirituals. Viking. (1)
Kennedy: *Black Cameos*. Boni. (1)
    Mellows. Boni. (1)
Kerlin: *Negro Poets and Their Poems*. Associated Publishers. (1, 2, 3)
Krehbiel: *Afro-American Folk-Songs*. Schirmer. (1)
Locke: *The New Negro*, pp. 3-47, 199-213. Boni. (1, 2, 3)
McNeill: *Lyrics from Cotton Land*. Stone. (3)
Niles: *Singing Soldiers*. Scribner. (1)
Odum and Johnson: *The Negro and His Songs*. U. N. C. Press. (1)
    Negro Workaday Songs. U. N. C. Press. (1)
Page: *In Ole Virginia*. Scribner. (3)
Scarborough: *On the Trail of Negro Folk Songs*. Harvard Press. (1)
Talley: *Negro Folk Rhymes*. Macmillan. (1)
Taylor and Ballanta: *St. Helena Island Spirituals*. Schirmer. (1)
White: *American Negro Folk-Songs*. Harvard Press. (1)
White and Jackson: *An Anthology of Verse by American Negroes*. Duke
    University Press. (1, 2, 3)
Work, F. J.: *Some American Negro Songs*. Boston. 1909.
Work, J. W.: *Folk Songs of the American Negro*. Fisk. (1)

MAGAZINES

Bookman, 63: 122, March, 1926. (1)
Journal of American Folk-Lore, 35: 223, 1922. (1)
Opportunity, 4: 158, May, 1926. (1)
    3: 330-336, November, 1925. (1)
    1: 292, October, 1923. (1)
Southern Workman, 243-247, May, 1918. (1)
    172-176, April, 1918. (1)
    563-565, December, 1925. (1)
    238-245, April, 1912. (1)

CHAPTER II

CONTEMPORARY POETRY

F<small>OLLOWING</small> Dunbar there sprang up among Negro and white writers, a sort of school of dialect poetry, generally depicting the Negro peasant type and adding little new to the accepted tradition of Southern plantation life. But among the Negroes the feeling has been growing that such performances were primarily entertainment for the "white folks" and not to be considered as literature. And with increased educational and economic advantages the race has evolved its own audience of readers, while an intellectual background has given the Negro poet a more sophisticated view of his medium. In developing their individual gifts some few writers have avoided any expression of racial consciousness, confining themselves entirely to themes of general appeal and traditional form. On the other hand, an intense consciousness of race discrimination has caused some of the best colored writers to protest with passionate and biting invective—sometimes more propaganda than poetry.

Uneven in quality but most promising of new contributions is the work of a small body of modernists, conscious of their race as an asset in their art and restlessly seeking the freshest, least conventional forms for the expression of what is universal in their experience and their inheritance.

Subjects for Study

1. A G<small>ENERAL</small> S<small>URVEY</small>

a. A consideration of the dialect verse of Alex Rogers, Daniel Webster Davis, James Edwin Campbell, Ray G. Dandridge, J. Mord Allen, John Wesley Holloway.
   1. Notice the influence of Paul Laurence Dunbar.
   2. Discuss the type of Negro portrayed in these verses. Compare the type found in the stories of Thomas Nelson Page and Joel Chandler Harris and in the dialect poetry of such writers as John Charles McNeill.
   3. Compare Claude McKay's use of West Indian dialect in "Two-an-Six." Note the dialect differences with varying localities, as shown in the work of the writers studied.

4. Compare the use of modified dialect in James Weldon Johnson's "The Creation."
b. The poetry of Benjamin Brawley, Leslie Pinckney Hill, Georgia Douglas Johnson, George Marion McClellan, James D. Corrothers, Jessie Fauset, Joseph S. Cotter, Sr.
  1. Note the rather conventional choice of subject matter and use of verse forms, the absence of racial self-consciousness in the best work of these writers.

2. Spokesmen for the Race

a. Poetry of protest, from the time of the anti-slavery agitators to Dunbar. Contrast the bitterness of many lesser poets with his expression of race aspiration.
b. Revolt against race discrimination, especially since the World War.
  Roscoe C. Jamison—"The Negro Soldiers."
  Joseph Seaman Cotter, Jr.—"Sonnet to Negro Soldiers," "Is It Because I Am Black?", "And What Shall You Say?"
  Fenton Johnson—"The New Day."
  James D. Corrothers—"At the Closed Gate of Justice."
c. Indignation over the lynching of Negroes.
  Leslie Pinckney Hill—"So Quietly."
  W. E. B. DuBois—"A Litany of Atlanta."
  Paul Laurence Dunbar—"The Haunted Oak."
  Compare the poems of two white writers, William Ellery Leonard's "The Lynching Bee" and Ridgely Torrence's "The Bird and the Tree." Read carefully "Brothers," by James Weldon Johnson, probably the fairest statement of the problem by a Negro.
d. The more constructive view of the problem has fostered a strong race pride and substituted for shame at former slavery a belief in the cleansing power of suffering and determination to work a way upwards for the race.
  Leslie Pinckney Hill—"The Wings of Oppression," "Tuskegee," "Freedom," "Self-Determination."
  J. Mord Allen—"The Psalm of Uplift."
  Fenton Johnson—"Children of the Sun."
  James Weldon Johnson—"Fifty Years," "O Southland."
e. Realization of the opportunity of the Negro as artist.
  James Weldon Johnson—"O Black and Unknown Bards."
  Charles Bertram Johnson—"Negro Poets."
  James D. Corrothers—"The Road to the Bow," "The Negro Singer."

3. Modernists

a. Consider briefly the "Black Renaissance" in the arts. Note the general tendencies of Negro musicians, writers, and artists to experiment as does the white modernist.

b. The "new Negro" shows his mental attitude toward his race in his choice of subject matter and mode of treatment. Interest in his African inheritance and primitive arts is a distinct new note.
c. Consider the growing interest in poetry, the number of Negro writers of creditable magazine verse. Review their contributions in national magazines such as *The Century, The American Mercury, The Atlantic Monthly*, etc., and in the Negro magazines, *The Crisis* and *Opportunity*, the Negro poets' number of *Palms*, the poetry sections of *The New Negro, Ebony and Topaz*, and the Negro numbers of *The Carolina Magazine*. Note the experimental issuing of a literary quarterly, *Fire*, and a poetry magazine, *Black Opals*.
d. Study the free verse experiments of Fenton Johnson, Joseph Seaman Cotter, Jr., Angelina Grimke, Anne Spencer, Jean Toomer, other younger writers, Gwendolyn Bennett, Lewis Alexander, Arna Bontemps, Helene Johnson.
   1. Form. Experiment with new metrical effects, emphasis on pattern, efforts to secure the inflection of colloquial speech.
   2. Diction. Vivid images, fresh and often bizarre expressions.
   3. Subject matter. Compare with the material of white writers in the new school of poetry. The best of the Negro writers attempt to make their works individual expressions, but they are not forgetful of their peculiar racial gifts in their striving to make a distinctive contribution to American art. Note reference to African inheritance, the use of religious motives as in "The Band of Gideon," by J. S. Cotter, Jr. Compare with Dr. E. C. L. Adams' "His Day is Done," a successful attempt by a white man to realize and describe a distinctly Negro emotion.
   4. Strength and weakness. Delight in decoration sometimes degenerates to over-ornateness, genius for striking images and intoxication with the sound of words lead to meaningless incoherence, and a bent for the dramatic sometimes suffers from lack of restraint.
e. Note the large number of writers of poetry. Estimate the value of this movement and the probability of its continuance and growth. Is the present interest in things Negro likely to be a passing vogue or a true "Black Renaissance"?

REFERENCES

(Numerals refer to subjects)

Adams: *Congaree Sketches*. U. N. C. Press. (2, 3)
Braithwaite: *Anthologies of Magazine Verse*, 1913—. Brimmer. (1, 2, 3)
Brawley: *The Negro in Literature and Art*. Duffield. (1, 2, 3)
Cullen: *Caroling Dusk*. Harper. (1, 2, 3)
Detweiler: *The Negro Press in the United States*. Univ. of Chicago. (1, 2, 3)

DuBois: *The Gift of Black Folk.* Stratford. (1, 2)
Gaines: *The Southern Plantation.* Columbia Press. (1)
Harris: *Uncle Remus, His Songs and His Sayings.* Appleton. (1)
Johnson, C. S. (ed.): *Ebony and Topaz.* Nat. Urban League. (2, 3)
Johnson, J. W.: *The Book of American Negro Poetry.* Harcourt. (1, 2, 3)
Kerlin: *Negro Poets and Their Poems.* Associated Publishers. (1, 2, 3)
Leonard: *The Lynching Bee.* Viking. (2)
Locke: *Four Negro Poets.* Simon and Schuster. (3)
   The New Negro, pp. 3-53, 254-271, 136-153. Boni. (1, 2, 3)
McNeill: *Lyrics from Cotton Land.* Stone. (1)
Monroe and Henderson: *The New Poetry.* Macmillan. (2, 3)
Page: *In Ole Virginia.* Scribner. (1, 2, 3)
Toomer: *Cane.* Boni and Liveright. (3)
Untermeyer: *American Poetry Since 1900.* Holt. (1, 2, 3)
White and Jackson: *An Anthology of Verse by American Negroes.* Duke
   Univ. Press. (1, 2, 3)
Wood: *Poets of America.* Dutton.

MAGAZINES

Black Opals, any issue.
Carolina Magazine, May, 1927, and May, 1928. (1, 2, 3)
Crisis, April, 1919. (1, 2, 3)
Fire, any issue.
Opportunity, 5: 108-110, April, 1927. (3)
   4: 146-160, May, 1926. (3)
   6: 146. May, 1928.
Palms, October, 1926. "The Negro Renaissance." (1, 2, 3)
Southern Workman, 56: 177, April, 1927.
Survey, 53: March 1, 1925. Harlem number. (1, 2, 3)

CHAPTER III

THREE LEADING POETS

IF we omit the names of Hughes and Cullen, the most brilliant of the younger poets, Braithwaite, Johnson, and McKay appear as the outstanding figures in the field of poetry. The first two also stand as critics, Braithwaite's work not being confined to the limits of race. His own poetry is important to this study not because of any racial characteristics, but because of his high attainment in methods and subject matter identical with that of a white writer.

James Weldon Johnson, a leader of his people in many activities, has made a notable contribution in the field of criticism, both literary and musical. His poetry follows traditional forms except as he experiments in the use of a modified dialect to convey the Biblical phrasings and the rhythms of the Negro folk-sermon.

Claude McKay's lyrics are conventionally romantic in treatment and sometimes in theme. But he has been one of the first to give voice to the new spirit among Negro artists, a mystical merging of individual identity with that of the race, pride in Africa's past, tenderness for all Negroes, bitterness for all who oppress them, and a defiance which mounts to flaming faith in the superiority of this people.

Subjects for Study

1. WILLIAM STANLEY BRAITHWAITE

a. Life, education, and training. Newspaper experience.
b. Work as an editor and compiler of standard collections of Elizabethan, Georgian, and Restoration verse. Criticism of contemporary poetry in his prefaces to his yearly anthologies of magazine verse, works which have an important place in encouraging contemporary writers and which have no reference to race.
c. Braithwaite's own poetry.
    1. The influence of Blake, Keats, Shelley.
    2. His philosophy stated in such poems as "This is My Life," "Sic Vita," "A Song of Living," "The Eternal Self."
    3. Estimate Braithwaite as a lyric poet, without regard to his race. Quote from "In a Graveyard," "By an Inland Lake," "Sandy Star."

2. JAMES WELDON JOHNSON

a. Early life and education. Collaboration with his brother in popularizing early rag-time songs, the forerunners of jazz. The two later worked together in collecting two volumes of spirituals. Their work has been a large factor in the present appreciation of Negro music. (See introductions to collections of poetry and spirituals and also *An Autobiography of an Ex-Coloured Man.*)
b. Work as a teacher, United States Consul in South America, and work for his race in America in various organizations.
c. Critical work. Editor of *The Book of American Negro Poetry.* A novel, *The Autobiography of an Ex-Coloured Man.*
d. Poetry. *Fifty Years and Other Poems* and *God's Trombones.*
   1. Note the form and the not unusual subject matter of "Fifty Years," "Mother Night," "O Black and Unknown Bards"; the restrained sincerity of treatment.
   2. Consider *God's Trombones* in detail, especially "The Creation" and "Go Down Death." Note the Biblical beauty of language which links them with the spiritual, the richness and homeliness of the imagery, the imaginative sweep. Compare Vachel Lindsay's experiments with Negro sermons, also Dr. Adams' *Congaree Sketches,* DuBose Heyward's *Jasbo Brown,* and similar poems by white writers.
   3. Discuss Johnson's use of modified dialect and his reasons for avoiding straight dialect. (See preface to *God's Trombones.*)
   4. Read one sermon.

3. CLAUDE MCKAY

a. Ancestry, life in Jamaica, early poetry and music. His studies in America, return to writing while earning a living by other means.
b. Editorial and journalistic work. Publication of *Harlem Shadows.* Travels abroad. Appearance of his verse in various magazines and publication of *Home to Harlem,* a novel.
   1. Love of nature, homesickness for Jamaica—"The Easter Flower," "Flame-Heart," "The Tropics in New York," "Subway Wind," "I Shall Return," "After the Winter."
   2. Beauty in the new country—"Spring in New Hampshire."
   3. The city touches his imagination—"Dawn in New York," "The Night Fire."
   4. Personal emotions. "My Mother" and some of the love poems such as "Absence" and "To O. E. A." are done with sincere simplicity. Others such as "Romance" and "Flirtations" achieve a studied sophistication. Contrast the oversensuousness of "Flower of Love."

c. Poems consciously or inherently racial.
   1. A sensing of primitive inheritance, nostalgia—"Outcast," "On a Primitive Canoe."
   2. In praise of the Negro's genius for song and dance—"Alfonso Dressing to Wait on Table," "Negro Dancers."
   3. Tenderness for individuals of his race, tinged with indignation over their condition—"Harlem Shadows," "The Harlem Dancer," "The Castaways."
   4. Race loyalty, defiance, bitterness—"Africa," "Enslaved," "The White City," "Birds of Prey," "If We Must Die," "The Lynching," "To the White Fiends."
   5. Oppression as a test of strength—"White Houses," "America," "In Bondage," "Baptism."

d. Estimate the strength and weakness of McKay's work.

REFERENCES
(Numerals refer to subjects)

Braithwaite: *Anthologies of Magazine Verse,* 1913—. (See 1925 issue) (1, 2, 3)
   The House of Falling Leaves. Luce. (1)
   Lyrics of Life and Love. Turner. (1)
Brawley: *The Negro in Literature and Art.* Duffield. (1, 2, 3)
Cullen: *Caroling Dusk.* Harper. (1, 2, 3)
DuBois: *The Gift of Black Folk.* Stratford. (1, 2, 3)
Heyward, DuBose, and Allen, Hervey: *Carolina Chansons.* Macmillan. (3)
Johnson: *The Autobiography of an Ex-Coloured Man.* Knopf.
   The Book of American Negro Poetry. Harcourt. (1, 2, 3)
   Fifty Years and Other Poems. Viking. (2)
   God's Trombones. Viking. (2)
Johnson and Johnson: *The Book of American Negro Spirituals.* Viking. (2)
   The Second Book of American Negro Spirituals. Viking. (2)
Kerlin: *Negro Poets and Their Poems.* Associated Publishers. (1, 2, 3)
Lindsay: *Collected Poems.* Macmillan. (2)
Locke: *Four Negro Poets.* Simon and Schuster. (3)
   The New Negro, pp. 3-53, 133, 138-141, 214. Boni. (1, 2, 3)
McKay: *Harlem Shadows.* Harcourt. (3)
   Home to Harlem. Harper. (3)
Monroe and Henderson: *The New Poetry.* Macmillan. (3)
Ovington: *Portraits in Color.* Viking. (2)
Untermeyer: *American Poetry Since 1900.* Holt. (1, 2, 3)
White and Jackson: *An Anthology of Verse by American Negroes.* Duke Univ. Press. (1, 2, 3)
Wood: *Poets of America.* Dutton. (1, 2, 3)

MAGAZINES

American Mercury, 10: 394. Johnson's "Go Down Death." (2)
    6:7-9, September, 1925. Heyward's "Jasbo Brown." (2)
Bookman, 55: 531, July, 1922. (3)
Century, 113: 682, 1927. Johnson's "Judgment Day." (2)
Crisis. See files.
Independent, 109: 54, August 5, 1922. (3)
Nation, 114: 694, June 7, 1922. (3)
New Republic, 31: 196, July 12, 1922. (3)
Opportunity, May, 1928, p. 151. See files.
Palms, October, 1926. "The Negro Renaissance." (1, 2, 3)
Southern Workman, 55: 371, 1926. Words of Johnson's "Lift up your Voice and Sing"; music from Theodore Presser Company, Philadelphia. (2)
Survey, 53: March 1, 1925. Harlem number. (1, 2, 3)

CHAPTER IV

TWO YOUNGER POETS

Countee Cullen and Langston Hughes have commanded attention among present day writers, not because of race but on account of the quality of their work, and because they give voice to the general revolt of modern youth. Their work expresses a recklessness and abandon which cover a deep sense of hurt and disillusion, and a hardness and sophistication which mask youth's pity. They have learned the use of irony in dealing with injustice. Their experience as Negroes furnishes them with emotions and sensations of universal appeal, and they are not limited by the racial point of view. Their work is distinctly individual. In form, Langston Hughes has been a rebel. Though his experiments have not been uniformly happy he merits attention for his use of new rhythms to convey the inflection and the flavor of Negro speech and for the life and color of his poems. Countee Cullen's work is not so bizarre; it is more intellectual and of more even quality. In the work of both there is a freedom, a sophistication, and a sureness which indicate an uprooting of any feeling of inferiority and a consequent mental balance and detachment not seen in the work of earlier poets.

Subjects for Study

1. Countee Cullen

a. Short sketch of his life, education, early writing, prize awards in competitions open to both white and Negro writers. Note that his first honor was won while a high school student and his first volume published at the age of twenty-two. This precocity would have been impossible without intellectual opportunities denied earlier Negro writers.

b. Editorial work. Negro poets' number of *Palms* and work as assistant editor of *Opportunity*. Anthology, *Caroling Dusk*.

c. First poetry influenced by younger white poets, particularly Edna St. Vincent Millay.

    1. Compare his "Shroud of Color" with "Renascence" of Millay. Note Cullen's lack of quaint charm. The greater exuberance of his imagery sometimes amounts to confusion. He has more solemnity and less mystical ecstasy, less skill in handling metre than Millay.

  2. Compare "Fruit of the Flower" with Millay's "The Singing-Woman from the Wood's Edge."
  3. Recklessness, sense of the transiency of love, delight in beauty—"She of the Dancing Feet Sings," "To a Brown Girl," "To a Brown Boy," "Harlem Wine," "To One Who Said Me Nay," "To You Who Read My Books."
  4. Pessimism, revolt against conventional religion—"The Wise," "Suicide Chant," "Gods."
d. His faults are largely those of youth. His strongest points are:
  1. Gift for epigrammatic expression at its best in his epitaphs and in portrait studies such as "A Brown Girl Dead" and "Caprice." Note the humor of "To My Fairer Brethren," "For a Lady I Know," "For a Mouthy Woman."
  2. Lyric expression of a mood—"If You Should Go," "Spring Reminiscence."
  3. Note the singing quality of many lines, the effective handling of metre and rhyme, the fresh and imaginative imagery; quote from his sonnets such as "An Old Story."
  4. A masculine strength which even in pessimistic mood does not lapse into pettiness.
e. He has given an individual expression to emotions and experiences of his race.
  1. Compare him to McKay in his sensing of primitive heritage, feeling in himself a reincarnation of the jungle—"Brown Boy to a Brown Girl," "Atlantic City Waiter," "The Dance of Love," "Heritage."
  2. Revolt from the inconsistencies of modern creeds to a deeper and simpler religion—"Simon the Cyrenian Speaks," "Black Magdalens," "Pagan Prayer."
  3. As regards race discrimination, he never descends to propaganda but cools his indignation and sharpens it with irony, a new and powerful note in Negro poetry. Read "Yet Do I Marvel," and "Incident."
f. Consider his expression of the universality of art, especially in "Extenuation to Certain Critics." (*Ebony and Topaz.*)
g. Review *Copper Sun*, noting particularly the sonnets.

2. Langston Hughes

a. Short sketch of his life, education. Prize awards.
b. Particularly in his free verse Hughes shows the influence of Carl Sandburg, Vachel Lindsay, and others. Notice his use of jazz rhythms and colloquial phrasing, the shouting color, vivid images, the striving after new and unused verse schemes. Read "Suicide's Note," "Winter Moon," "Seascape," "Sea Calm," "When Sue Wears Red," "An Earth Song."

c. His jazz pieces his most original contribution—humor, abandon, recklessness without self-consciousness. Read "Jazzonia," "Nude Young Dancer," "The Weary Blues," "To Midnight Nan at Leroy's," "Song for a Banjo Dance," "Blues Fantasy." Compare the folk-song blues and jazz verses.
   d. Poems of racial consciousness.
   1. Mystic identification with the past of his race. Read "The Negro Speaks of Rivers," "Dream Variation," "Our Land," "Afraid," "Proem," "Lament for Dark Peoples," "Danse Africaine."
   2. Self-pity in "Black Pierrot," "Cross," "Minstrel Man." Compare "The Jester."
   3. Bitterness and protest in "As I Grow Older," "The South," "The White Ones."
   4. Race pride, a summons for the future—"Epilogue" ("I, Too, Sing America"), "Youth" ("We Have Tomorrow"), "Poem" ("Being Walkers with the Dawn and Morning"), "Song" ("Lovely, Dark and Lonely One").
   e. Chief faults of Hughes' work. Note the uneven quality. Some of his pieces are trite and even sentimental, others strain grotesquely for an effect. Compare him with Cullen for ability in self-criticism.
   f. Study any other poems available in magazines, collections, or in *Fine Clothes to the Jew*. Estimate the value of Hughes' present contribution, the probable effect of his innovations on the poetry of younger writers, white and colored.
   (NOTE: All the poems selected for study will be found in Hughes' *The Weary Blues*, with the exception of "An Earth Song," "Being Walkers with the Dawn and Morning," "Minstrel Man," "Lovely, Dark and Lonely One." These will be found in *The New Negro*.
   If a third subject is desired, *Fine Clothes to the Jew*, *Copper Sun*, and other recent poetry of these writers may be made the subject of separate review, selections also being read.)

REFERENCES

(Numerals refer to subjects)

Adams: *Congaree Sketches*. U. N. C. Press. (1, 2)
Braithwaite: *Anthology of Magazine Verse*, 1926. Brimmer. (1, 2)
Cullen: *Caroling Dusk*. Harper.
    Color. Harper.
    Copper Sun. Harper.
Handy: *Blues*. Boni.
Hughes: *Fine Clothes to the Jew*. Knopf.
    The Weary Blues. Knopf.
Johnson, C. S. (ed.): *Ebony and Topaz*. Nat. Urban League. (2, 3)
Johnson, J. W.: *The Book of American Negro Poetry*.

Lindsay: *Collected Poems.* Macmillan. (2)
Locke: *Four Negro Poets.* Simon and Schuster. (1, 2)
   The New Negro, pp. 2-53, 216-224, 129-133, 141-146, 226-227, 250. Boni. (1, 2)
Millay: *Renascence.* Kennerley. (1)
Niles: *Singing Soldiers.* Scribner. (2)
Ovington: *Portraits in Color.* Viking. (2)
Untermeyer: *American Poetry Since 1900.* Holt. (1, 2)
Wood: *Poets of America.* Dutton. (1, 2)

MAGAZINES

Black Opals. See files. (1, 2)
Bookman, 62: 503, December, 1925. (1)
Books, February 20, 1927. (2)
Carolina Magazine, May, 1927. (1, 2) May, 1928. (1, 2, 3)
Crisis. See files.
Independent, 115: 539, November 7, 1925. (1)
Nation, 121: 763, December 30, 1925. (1)
   122: 692-694, June 23, 1926. (1, 2)
   124: 403, April 13, 1927. (2)
New Republic, 46: 371-372, May 12, 1926. (2)
   51: 76-77, June 8, 1927. (2)
   46: 179, March 31, 1926. (1)
Opportunity, 4: 14, 72, 73, 146-160, 257, 381-382, 1926. (1, 2)
   5: 84-86, 108-110, 270-271, 1927. (1, 2)
Palms, October, 1926. (1, 2)
Poetry, 28: 50-53, 1926. (1)
Saturday Review, 3: 712, April 9, 1927. (2)
Southern Workman, 56: 177, April, 1927. (1, 2)

PART II. DRAMA

CHAPTER V

THE NEGRO'S CONTRIBUTION TO THE ART OF THE THEATRE

IN the writing of plays for the American stage the work of the Negro has, up to the present, been almost negligible. He has lacked not only the experience and background but the audience for what he might write. And his artistic viewpoint has been too self-conscious for this—one of the most objective forms of literature. The plays by Negroes are important largely as indications of what may develop. But the race has already influenced the art of the stage in America through acting, music, and dances. Some fine actors have interpreted rôles created for them by white writers. Others, especially the comedians, have had a hand in creating new forms, such as the musical comedy and the minstrel show. Whatever we may think of these forms, we must admit their distinctive Americanism and the possibilities for their greater and more artistic development. The many struggling groups of Negro players are giving their actors a chance to interpret Negro parts in plays written for them and are looking forward to the maturing of the art of the Negro playwright, furnishing an audience, a means of production, and a stimulating demand for material.

Subjects for Study

1. THE GIFT OF SONG AND DANCE

a. Early ragtime, its origin among the Southern Negroes, introduction on the stage in Chicago and New York. Characteristically Negro in words and music. Comment on the folk-character of the Blues, ballads, and songs.
b. Gradual absorption into American life to become popular music of the nation. Nature of jazz. Its interpretation of one phase of America.
c. Possibilities for the development of jazz.
d. The cake walk, which swept this country and Europe, gave rise to other dances distinctly Negro in origin but American, as is the Negro of today. Note the present vogue of Negro dancers abroad.
e. Song and dance on the stage.
   1. Early "minstrel shows," copying the antics of the slaves.
   2. Negro comedy entertainers, interpreting their race according to the white man's ideas.

3. Negro musical comedies such as *Shuffle Along*.
4. Musical comedy's debt to the Negro.
5. Negro revues and primitive dances.
6. Influence on more serious music.

f. Estimate the value of this contribution.

2. Negro Actors

a. Discuss the difficulties of the Negro because of the early dearth of parts open to him.
b. Comedians.
    1. Bert Williams, Florence Mills.
    2. Other musical comedy stars and famous teams.
c. Ira Aldridge. His work in serious drama, recognition abroad.
d. Charles Gilpin. His early training in comedy and rise to prominence in *The Emperor Jones*.
e. Paul Robeson. A sketch of his career. The scarcity of suitable plays has caused him to devote most of his time to concert work with Negro spirituals.
f. Other Negro men and women on the stage.
    1. Arthur Hopkins' production of the opera *Deep River* discovered Julius Bledsoe and Rose McClendon, who later appeared in Paul Green's *In Abraham's Bosom*.
    2. Sketch the career of Frank Wilson.
    3. Note that until recently only experimental groups have been interested in trying out plays with all-Negro casts, small incidental parts being all the colored actor could look for in the commercial theatre.
g. Discuss the possible effect on the drama of the increased interest in the Negro spiritual and in Negro art.

3. Negro Playwrights

a. Experimental theatres established to encourage writers and actors of the race.
    1. Sketch the work of the Hapgood Players, The Chicago Ethiopian Art Theatre and Shadows Art Theatre, the Krigwa Little Theatres of New York and Washington. Note the early scarcity of dramas of Negro life and the success of the Krigwa Players with such material as *The Fool's Errand* of Eulalie Spence.
    2. Drama in the college. The work of Montgomery Gregory with the Howard University Players encouraged Negro playwrights. Note the increase of college groups, the Hampton Players, Gilpin and Robeson Players.
    3. Other dramatic enterprises, stock companies such as the Lafayette Players of Harlem. Pageants such as DuBois' *Star of Ethiopia*.

b. Discuss the reasons for lack of success in earlier plays by Negroes. Those who attempted this form have usually made it a vehicle for ideas presented in a self-conscious manner. Angelina Grimke's *Rachel* is an example.

c. Note the encouragement offered by *The Crisis* and *Opportunity* prize contests. Summarize some of these prize plays.

d. Discuss the plays by Negroes in Locke and Gregory, *Plays of Negro Life,* particularly those of Willis Richardson, Georgia Douglas Johnson, and Eulalie Spence. Comment on the note of humor and irony introduced by Miss Spence, the color and fire in some of the imaginative pieces.

e. Study particularly *Plumes,* by Georgia Douglas Johnson. Note the swift and penetrating characterization. Criticize the craftsmanship displayed in dealing with the ending of the play. This drama omits any emphasis on race but deals with a common human situation.

REFERENCES
(Numerals refer to subjects)

Brawley: *The Negro in Literature and Art.* Duffield. (1, 2, 3)
Detweiler: *The Negro Press in the United States.* Univ. of Chicago. (2)
DuBois: *The Gift of Black Folk.* Stratford. (1, 2, 3)
Gaines: *The Southern Plantation.* Columbia Univ. Press. (1, 2)
Grimke: *Rachel.* Cornhill. (3)
Handy: *Blues.* Boni. (1)
Johnson, G. D.: *Plumes.* French. Also in *Plays of Negro Life.*
Johnson, J. W.: *The Book of American Negro Poetry.* Harcourt. (1)
Locke: *The New Negro,* pp. 153-168; 168-195; 216-195. Boni. (1, 2, 3)
Locke and Gregory: *Plays of Negro Life.* Harper. (3)
Odum and Johnson: *Negro Workaday Songs.* U. N. C. Press. (1)
Ovington: *Portraits in Color.* Viking (2)
Rowland: *Bert Williams, Son of Laughter.* English Crafters. (2)
Seldes: *The Seven Lively Arts.* Harper. (1, 2)
Sergeant: *Fire Under the Andes.* Knopf. (2)
Shay: *Fifty More Contemporay One-Act Plays.* Appleton.
Spence: *The Fool's Errand.* French. (3)
Toomer: *Cane.* Boni and Liveright.

MAGAZINES

American Magazine, 70: 600-604, September, 1910. (2)
    85: 33-35, January, 1918. (2)
American Mercury, 1: 243-244, 1924. (2)
    2: 371-372, 1924. (2)
    2: 113-115, 1924. (2)
    9: 500-502, 1926. (2)
    11: 395-398, 1927. (1, 2)

Atlantic, November, 1867. (1)
         July, 1869. (1)
Carolina Magazine, May, 1927. (12)
Crisis, August, 1916, p. 169 (1, 2)
         November, 1919. (3)
         34: 85-103; 229; 248, 1927.
         April, 1927. (2)
         See also files for contest awards, etc.
Drama, 16: 54, November, 1925. (2)
         16: 224, March, 1926. (2)
Harper's, 79, January and June, 1889. (1, 2)
Literary Digest, 48: 1114, May 9, 1914. (2)
         72: 28-29, March 25, 1922. (2)
         June 10, 1911. (1, 2)
Munsey, May, 1908. (1, 2)
Nation, 116: 605-606, May 23, 1923. (2)
         118: 664, June 4, 1924. (2)
New Republic, 28: 350, 1921. (2)
         46: 40-44, 1926. (2)
Opportunity, 1: 20, April, 1923. (2)
         3: 346, November, 1925. (2)
         4: 181, 357, 388-396, 1926. (1, 2)
         5: 53, 86, 87, 90, 336-339, 1927. (2, 3)
         6: 90, 122, 153, 166, 180, 214, 1928.
Scribner's, June, 1915. (1)
Theatre Arts Monthly, 10: 112-120, February, 1926. (1, 2)
         10: 701-706, October, 1926. (3)
         11: 282-293, April, 1927. (1, 2)

CHAPTER VI

DRAMA FOR NEGRO ACTORS

Discounting as propaganda the early slave romances such as *The Octoroon* and *Uncle Tom's Cabin,* and passing over Sheldon's *The Nigger* as essentially a white man's view of the miscegenation problem, we recognize Ridgely Torrence as the first writer to see the dramatic material in Negro life and character and to reproduce it on the stage with Negro actors. Coming at a time when the Irish dramatists had demonstrated the appeal of folk drama, this experiment might have led to the establishment, by Torrence and other white artists, of a permanent Negro theatre. But the World War intervened. Since then the young Negroes have attempted to stand on their own feet. Until now their experimental groups have been short lived, though some interesting work has been done, but there is a growing number of plays written for Negro actors and available to such groups and to stock companies. Ernest Culbertson's *Goat Alley* is a realistic tragedy of Negro life written by a white man who viewed these characters as material for art and depicted them truly without regard for problem or propaganda. His tragedy was produced by Negro actors, the first of such full length plays to attain any measure of success.

Subjects for Study

1. Negro Life—Material for White Dramatists

a. The sentimentality and unreality of slave tragedies. *The Octoroon* and *Uncle Tom's Cabin.*
b. Sheldon's *The Nigger,* its plot, production, and significance.
c. Ridgely Torrence's folk plays, *Granny Maumee* and *The Rider of Dreams.*
   1. Discuss the point of view of the dramatist. Note the absence of propaganda, the interest in character, the poetic use of dialect. The Negro appeals to Torrence as fresh vital material.
   2. Sketch the plot of *The Rider of Dreams.*
   3. The production of Torrence's bill of one-act plays and the interest aroused.

2. "Granny Maumee"

a. The characters. Consider Granny Maumee, to whom the other women are merely foils. Is she convincing? Compare the old woman in George Madden Martin's *The Lion's Mouth*.
b. The plot. Note the swift exposition, economical means of explaining the past. Discuss the plausibility of Granny Maumee's sudden change from hatred to forgiveness. Is it dramatically effective and convincing?
c. Criticise the play. Is Torrence primarily a dramatist or a poet?
d. Read part of the play, preferably the enchantment scene.

3. Ernest Culbertson's "Goat Alley"

a. The dramatist's interest in his material. It is not the pathos of the Negro's condition, but the trials of Lucy Belle and her tragedy which appeal to him. Note the many phases of Negro life in city slums. Culbertson succeeds in making them an organic part of the play. Compare his point of view with that of Carl Van Vechten in *Nigger Heaven*, where exposition overbalances the artistic unity of the story. Discuss the opinion of certain race leaders that the tragic treatment of peasant types gives "greater currency to the popular notion of the Negro as an inferior, superstitious, half ignorant, and servile class of folk."
b. Discuss the plot of *Goat Alley*. Compare with the one-act version.
   Is the tragic climax built up so that the action of Lucy Belle seems inevitable?
c. The characters. Are they alive and convincing? Note the dialogue and compare with that of *Granny Maumee*.
d. The production of *Goat Alley* in New York with Negro actors. Note such folk-plays as *Roseanne* and the Broadway productions of *Black Boy* and *Lulu Belle*, the latter a popular success.
e. The value of Culbertson's work.

REFERENCES

(Numerals refer to subjects)

Boucicault: *The Octoroon*. (See Quinn's *Representative American Plays*.) Century. (1)
Brawley: *The Negro in Literature and Art*. Duffield. (1, 2, 3)
Culbertson: *Goat Alley*. Appleton. (3) (Also Shay's *Twenty Contemporary One-Act Plays*.)
DuBois: *The Gift of Black Folk*. Stratford.
Gaines: *The Southern Plantation*. Columbia Univ. Press.
Locke: *The New Negro*, pp. 29-43, 153-160. Boni. (1, 2, 3)
Locke and Gregory: *Plays of Negro Life*. Harper. (1, 2, 3)

Moses: *Representative Plays by American Dramatists,* vol. II. (Stowe's "Uncle Tom's Cabin" by George Aiken). Dutton. (1)
Quinn: *Representative American Plays* (Boucicault's "Octoroon"). Century. (1)
Shay: *Twenty Contemporary One-Act Plays—American* (Culbertson's "Goat Alley"). Appleton. (3)
Sheldon: *The Nigger.* Macmillan. (1)
Smith: *Short Plays by Representative Authors* (Torrence's "The Rider of Dreams"). Macmillan. (1)
Stowe: *Uncle Tom's Cabin* (dramatization). French. (1) (Also Moses' *Representative Plays.*)
Torrence: *Granny Maumee, The Rider of Dreams, Simon the Cyrenian.* Macmillan. (1 ,2, 3) (Also for "The Rider of Dreams" see Moses' *Representative Plays.*)
Van Vechten: *Nigger Heaven.* Knopf. (3)

MAGAZINES

American Mercury, 1: 243-244, 1924. (3)
    2: 271-372, July, 1924. (3)
    9: 500-50, Dec., 1926. (3)
Current Opinion, 62: 428-329, May, 1917.
Dial, 63: 529, November 22, 1917. (1, 2)
    49: 522, December 16, 1910. (1, 2)
Independent, 92: 63, October 6, 1917. (1, 2)
Literary Digest, 48: 1114, May 9, 1914. 1, 2)
Nation, 91: 272, September 22, 1910. (1)
New Republic, 10: 325, April 14, 1917. (1, 2)
Opportunity, 1: February, 1923. (3)
    3: February, 1925. (3)
    4: April, 1926. (3)
    5: February, 1927. (3)
Review of Reviews, 56: 444, October, 1917. (1, 2)
Theatre Arts Monthly, 10: 701-706, October, 1926. (1, 2, 3)
    10: 112-120, February, 1926. (1, 2, 3)

CHAPTER VII

THE NEGRO PLAYS OF EUGENE O'NEILL

Because he finds dramatic the lives of simple, unsophisticated folk, Eugene O'Neill has seen a wealth of drama in the Negro race. It is a tribute to the variety and richness of Negro life as well as to the author's originality that his three plays of the black man are so dissimilar. *The Dreamy Kid* is a realistic one-act study of a Negro criminal and his capture at the death-bed of his old grandmother. *The Emperor Jones* is a drama in which fear becomes a protagonist, working on the mind of the charlatan emperor to uncover his experiences of terror and also those of his race embodied in him. *All God's Chillun Got Wings* is more tragic in intent though not entirely successful dramatically. O'Neill in this play held no thesis concerning the intermarriage of whites and blacks. He saw and depicted two human beings caught by a passion stronger than their inherited and instinctive inhibitions and defeated because these very racial traits in their natures would permit no happiness in a union. The individuals—and their tragedy as individuals—are the one concern of this piece. The forces which crush them are the hatred and prejudice of both races and the shrinking and torture of the characters themselves in facing the problem. In such a struggle O'Neill has recognized the materials of tragedy.

Subjects for Study

1. The Material of O'Neill's Plays

a. Sketch O'Neill's early life and adventures at sea.
b. His first writings. Sketch briefly the literary career of this playwright from the early productions of the Provincetown Players.
c. The one-act sea plays in *The Moon of the Caribbees*. Note the type of seaman which interests O'Neill. Does he succeed in creating beauty out of the dirt and degradation of lowly folk, those close to the soil and the sea? Compare with other writers of folk-plays—Paul Green, for instance. Compare these one-act plays and *Anna Christie*, *Beyond the Horizon*, and *Desire under the Elms* with O'Neill's dramas of more sophisticated people, *Welded*, *The First Man*, *The Great God Brown*.

d. Note particularly *The Hairy Ape*, the first of a series of philosophical plays. Compare this and *The Fountain, Lazarus Laughed,* and *Marco Millions* with earlier realistic plays.
e. Summarize the different kinds of material with which O'Neill concerns himself. Note his tendency to experiment.
f. Estimate his place in dramatic literature.

2. "The Emperor Jones"

a. O'Neill's first experiment with the Negro, *The Dreamy Kid.* Compare, for skill in exposition, with *The Emperor Jones.* Note the device used in the first play to give information, namely, Dreamy's sister's ignorance of his day-old crime. Is this plausible? Compare the exposition in Paul Green's *The Prayer Meeting,* where the sub-plot is similar. Compare the characterization of *The Dreamy Kid* with *The Emperor Jones.* Note how natural to his character is the expository narrative of Jones in the first scene.
b. The form of *The Emperor Jones.* Note O'Neill's use of the soliloquy as a mechanical device. He made another innovation by abandoning the three or four-act form. Do his eight scenes gather up a sufficient accumulation of power, or might the ending be less expected? Note the tension at the end of *The Dreamy Kid.*
c. Characterization. Note the creation of atmosphere in the opening lines, the swift economical drawing of the figure of Smithers. Discuss Jones. Note how his uneasiness is hinted at under his bragging, then built up into terror through the recurring fears.
d. The building up of an impression of fear. Note the use of the tom-toms, the opportunities offered the producer for imaginative creation of scenery and light effects. Note the beauty of the simple dialect, the imaginative and yet characteristically Negroid figures and similes.
e. Discuss the play as a study of racial and subconscious fears. Is this sound psychology? Compare the conviction of the younger Negro poets of their mystical blood bond with the past, its primitive joys and fears. Estimate the importance of the play in O'Neill's development and in the freeing of the American drama from convention.

3. "All God's Chillun Got Wings"

a. The theme of the play. Before its production there were many attacks because of the central action, the union of a white woman and a Negro. In reality this resembles *The Emperor Jones* in that it is a study of effects upon individuals of racial fears, prejudices, and differences. The point of view is more human and the play more tragic.
b. The characters. O'Neill selected a weakling Negro and a coarse and spiritually undeveloped white girl. Why? Note the minor characters.

Contrast Shorty, Joe, and Mickey with Hattie and Mrs. Harris. Which is more convincing?

c. The plot. Note the delicacy with which O'Neill has handled a difficult action, the sureness with which he builds up a situation that, given the characters, leads to inevitable ruin. Their tragedy is the result not only of external forces but of flaws in the characters of each.

d. The form. Note the use of soliloquy, the number of scenes, the use of crowds of both races in the first act, and the narrowing to intimate scenes in the second.

e. The significance of this play.

REFERENCES

(Numerals refer to subjects)

Bechhofer: *The Literary Renaissance in America*. Heinnemann. (1, 2, 3)
Boynton: *Some Contemporary Americans*. Univ. of Chicago. (1, 2, 3)
Brawley: *The Negro in Literature and Art*. Duffield. (1, 2)
Clark: *Eugene O'Neill*. McBride. (1, 2, 3)
    A Study of the Modern Drama. Appleton. (1, 2, 3)
Dickinson: *Playwrights of the New American Theatre*. Macmillan. (1, 2, 3)
DuBois: *The Gift of Black Folk*. Stratford. (1, 2)
Hamilton: *Conversations on Contemporary Drama*. Macmillan. (1)
Locke: *The New Negro*, pp. 29-43, 153-160. Boni. (1, 2, 3)
Locke and Gregory: *Plays of Negro Life* ("Emperor Jones" and "The Dreamy Kid"). Harper. (1, 2, 3)
Moses: *Representative American Dramas* ("Emperor Jones"). Little. (2)
O'Neill: *All God's Chillun Got Wings* and *Welded*. Boni and Liveright. (3)
    Complete Works. Vol. II. Boni and Liveright. (1, 2, 3)
    1924.)
Quinn: *Contemporary American Plays*. ("Emperor Jones") Scribner. (2)
Sayler: *Our American Theatre*. Brentano (1, 2)
Sergeant: *Fire Under the Andes*. Knopf. (1)
Shay: *Twenty Contemporary One-Act Plays—American*. ("The Dreamy Kid"). Appleton. (2)

MAGAZINES

American Mercury, 1: 119, January, 1924.
    2: 113-115, 1924.
    9: 500-502, 1926.
    February, 1924 (O'Neill's "All God's Chillun Got Wings")
Freeman, 7: March 21, 1923. (1, 2)
Nation, March 22, 1922. (1)
    118-664, June 4, 1924. (1, 2, 3)
New Republic, November 15, 1922. (1)
    46, 197-198, April 7, 1926. (1, 2, 3)

Opportunity, 2: 369, December, 1924. (1, 2, 3)
        2: 113, April, 1924. (3)
        2: 221, July 1924. (3)
        3: 346, November, 1925. (2)
Theatre Arts Magazine, January, 1920. (O'Neill's "The Dreamy Kid.") (2)
        January, 1921. (O'Neill's "The Emperor Jones.") (2)
Theatre Arts Monthly, 8: 497, July, 1924. (1, 2, 3)
        10: 701-706, October, 1926. (1, 2, 3)

CHAPTER VIII

PAUL GREEN—INTERPRETER OF THE SOUTHERN NEGRO

Paul Green has been impelled to write of the Negro, not for sentimental reasons nor to start a movement to free the race from economic and social injustices, but because he is an artist looking for material and seeing beauty and tragedy in any deep and moving struggle of human beings. The Negro as Green has known him, sweating in the fields, shouting in religious ecstasy, brutal in his poverty and sin, or groping in his struggle after an idea—this Negro peasant exists as a human figure, a subject for comedy or tragedy to one who can interpret him in terms of his life. And this is what Paul Green attempts in his one-act and longer plays. Here are squalor and sin, ecstasy of religion or sex. Here are the sting of sweat, the music of simple emotion, laughter, homely speech, elements of a life growing out of the soil and returning to it in death. It is not simply a faithful picture of lowly folk which the author attempts. He sees the Negro struggling and the human significance of that struggle, the tragedy of its frequent defeat. He does not claim to give a representative picture of Negro life in America or even in the South. He interprets dramatically what appeals to him as moving in the life and characters with which he is familiar. The result is drama not bound to a narrow locality but measurable by the test of humanity.

Subjects for Study

1. SHORT PLAYS OF NEGRO LIFE

a. Early life and education, acquaintance with Negro life. Background for his plays.
b. Work with the Carolina Playmakers, productions of his one-act plays of white life. *White Dresses*, published in Lewis' *Contemporary One-Act Plays*, *Granny Boling* in *The Drama*, other Negro plays in *Poet Lore*. Production of *The No 'Count Boy* in Belasco Little Theatre Tournament. Publication of collected one-act plays in *The Lord's Will*.
c. Publication of *Lonesome Road*, a collection of one-act tragedies of Negro life. Note the reviews of these plays, particularly those of Negro reviewers.

d. Editing of *The Reviewer*. Attitude toward Southern literature and literary criticism.
e. Discuss *White Dresses* and *The End of the Row*. Note how the problem is subordinated to the character interest. The white men in each play are victims of the tragedy, not mere instruments of it. Compare Shands' handling of a similar problem in *White and Black*. Contrast the white villains of *The Fire in the Flint*.
f. *The Hot Iron*. Discuss this realistic study of poverty. Note the compactness of the action, skillful handling of exposition. Compare with plays in which the characters struggle for some central idea beyond their daily bread and a bare existence.
g. *The Prayer Meeting*. Note the brutal abandon of the piece, the juxtaposition and blending of sex and religion. Compare the episode of grandmother and criminal boy with O'Neill's handling of a similar situation in *The Dreamy Kid*.
h. Review briefly his other short Negro pieces, *Supper for the Dead, The Man Who Died at Twelve O'Clock, In the Valley, On the Road One Day, Lord,* and *In Aunt Mahaly's Cabin*. Compare his latest collection of one-act plays with *Lonesome Road*.
i. Paul Green's place among American Dramatists.

2. "THE NO 'COUNT BOY"

a. This is probably the best known of the one-act Negro plays. What is its appeal? Note its productions.
b. The plot. Sketch the action. Compare with Synge's *The Playboy of the Western World* and *The Shadow of the Glen*. Note how the plot grows out of the characterization—the comedy depending on character and not action. Note the preparation for the Boy's effect on Pheelie, her romantic and rebellious mood. Are her changes of heart convincing? Discuss the ending of the play.
c. The characters. Are they true to life? Note the contrasted characters of the two men. Does the author succeed in creating a portrait of the old woman in his few lines at the end?
d. Theme. One reason for the appeal of this play is that we have here two sides of a universal problem of living. Is either the practical or the romantic entirely triumphant?
e. Note the language of the play, the poetry in simple images and homely dialect. Note the use of music.
f. Read part of the Boy's description of his journeyings.

3. "IN ABRAHAM'S BOSOM"

a. Two one-act plays from *Lonesome Road* were the basis for this play. Describe the production with a Negro cast at the Provincetown Playhouse. Give a short account of the work of the Provincetown

Players, who have given a first hearing to O'Neill and others with whom Broadway could not afford to experiment.
b. Theme. Note the universal quality of the tragedy arising both from Abraham's own self-obsessions and from those obstacles which his race bequeathed him. Discuss the objections of certain Negro leaders that the black man should not be depicted as a failure. The author sees Abraham as a universally tragic figure when, at the climax of the play, he cries out to the ghosts of his parents that they should never have conceived him. So any human, utterly defeated, might cry out after a superhuman struggle.
c. The plot. Discuss the handling of the action. Is the scene method too novelistic or is there steadily increasing dramatic tension? Notice the treatment of the miscegenation element.
d. The characters. Discuss Abraham, his aunt, and wife. Note the swift characterization of the minor figures. Do they live? What is the purpose of the turpentine hands in the first scene? Compare their brutal comedy with that of *The Prayer Meeting*. Note also the comedy elements in the tragic scene at the school house and the scenes between Muh Mack and Douglas. Comment on the variety of the characters presented.
e. The language of the play. Note the use of the soliloquy in the closing scenes and compare with *The Emperor Jones*. Read the baptism prayer of Abraham.
f. Give a general estimate of the play. Comment on the award of the Pulitzer Prize and the attitude of critics toward the play.

REFERENCES

(Numerals refer to subjects)

American Caravan. ("Supper for the Dead" by Paul Green.) Macaulay. (1)
Clark, *The Writings of Paul Green.* McBride. (1, 2, 3)
Green: *The Field God* and *In Abraham's Bosom.* McBride. (3)
    In Aunt Mahaly's Cabin. French. (1)
    In the Valley. French. (1, 2)
    (Contains "In the Valley," "Quare Medicine," "The No 'Count Boy," "Unto Such Glory," "In Aunt Mahaly's Cabin," "The "Man Who Died at Twelve O'Clock," "Supper for the Dead," "The Man on the House," "The Picnic," "Saturday Night," "The Goodbye."
    Lonesome Road. McBride. (1, 2)
    (Contains "In Abraham's Bosom"—one act, "White Dresses," "The Hot Iron," "The Prayer Meeting," "The End of the Row," "Your Fiery Furnace."
    The Lord's Will. Holt. (1, 2)
    (Contains "The Lord's Will," "Blackbeard," "Old Wash Lucas,"

"The No 'Count Boy," "The Old Man of Edenton," "The Last of the Lowries."
The Man Who Died at Twelve O'Clock. French. (1)
Johnson: *Ebony and Topaz*. Nat. Urban League.
Lewis: *Contemporary One-Act Plays*. ("White Dresses.") Scribner. (1, 2)
Locke and Gregory: *Plays of Negro Life*. Harper. (1, 2, 3)
(Contains "The No 'Count Boy," "White Dresses," "In Abraham's Bosom.")

MAGAZINES

Arts and Decoration, April, 1927. (3)
Baltimore Evening Sun, November 16, 1926. Article by Addison Hibbard. (1, 2, 3)
Books (New York Herald Tribune), June 6, 1926. Review by Jessie Fauset.
(1, 2)
April 24, 1927. Review by Walter Pritchard Eaton. (3)
Boston Evening Transcript, May 5, 1927. (1, 2, 3)
Century, 112:510, August, 1926. (2, 3)
Commonweal, May 25, 1927. (3)
July 27, 1927. (1, 2, 3)
Crisis, 34: 12, March, 1927. Review by W. E. B. DuBois. (3)
Drama, 17: 136, 233, 1927. (2, 3)
Literary Digest, p. 21, May 28, 1927. (2, 3)
McCall's Magazine, 54: 27, September, 1927. (2, 3)
McClure's Magazine, August, 1927. (Note: There are many errors in this article, for example, the impression of educational institutions and attitudes toward them.)
Nation, 121: 485-486, October 28, 1925. (1, 2)
New Republic, 50: 46, March 2, 1927. (2, 3)
51: 260, July 27, 1927. (2, 3)
New York Evening Post, May 7, 1927. (Letter by Paul Green) (1, 2, 3)
New York Herald Tribune, December 31, 1926. Review by George Goldsmith. (3)
New York Times, Book Review Section, August 29, 1926. (1)
New York Times, December 31, 1926. (3)
January 9, 1927. (1, 2, 3)
May 8, 1927. Review by J. Brooks Anderson. April 15, 1928.
(1, 2, 3)
New York World, Book Review Section, April 17, 1927. Review by Walter White. (3)
Opportunity, 3: 121, April, 1925. (2)
3: 282, September, 1925. (1, 2, 3)
4: 294, September, 1926. (1, 2, 3)
4: 374-375, December, 1926. (1)
5: 54, February, 1927. (3)
5: 86, March, 1927. (3)

Raleigh News and Observer. January 9, 1927. Review by Ann Bridgers. (3)
    March 20, 1927. Article by Nell Battle Lewis. (1, 2, 3)
The Reviewer, all issues for 1925.
Saturday Review of Literature, pp. 781-783, May 15, 1926.
    pp. 940-941, July 2, 1927.
Survey, 57: 591, February 1, 1927. (2, 3)
Theatre Arts Monthly, 8: 773, November, 1924 ("The No 'Count Boy") (1)
    9: December, 1925. (1)
    10: 112-120, 701-706, 226-239, 1926. (1, 2)
    11: 170, 350, 390, 1927. (3)
Travel, June, 1927. (1, 2, 3)

PART III. FICTION

CHAPTER IX

THE "OLD-TIMEY" NEGRO AND HIS FOLK-LORE

Almost from the beginning of American literature, the Negro has had his place as material to be written of. At first he was the subject for slave novels, little more than tracts, and as lifeless as any sermon illustration. With the growth of the local color school the black man was discovered to be a romantic and picturesque figure. Such writers as Thomas Nelson Page, George W. Cable, and Joel Chandler Harris threw the pleasant haze of romance over the old plantation days, preserving a sentimentalized impression of the lighter side. And these writers, particularly Harris, were the means of preserving and popularizing a body of folk-lore and folk-tale which might otherwise have been lost.

Numerous collectors of today are stimulated, not by the appeal of the picturesque, but by the desire to make scientific record of folk-lore still surviving among the peasant class of southern Negroes. Of these, Ambrose Gonzales with his material from the Gullah country has made the bulkiest contribution. Dr. E. C. L. Adams in his *Congaree Sketches* has made more than a record. He has brought together conversations, scenes, and stories of great interest and presented them unbiased and unsentimentalized and yet with the human appeal always uppermost.

Subjects for Study

1. The Southern Plantation—A Romantic Legend

a. Early use of the Negro in fiction.
   1. As a lay figure in such stories as Cooper's *The Spy* and Poe's *The Gold Bug*. The character of the devoted slave.
   2. As the pathetic victim of slavery conditions in abolition novels such as *Uncle Tom's Cabin*.
b. American humor and dialect fiction.
   1. Mark Twain's use of the Negro. Note the use of dialect in *Pudd'nhead Wilson*. Page, Cable, and Harris aroused interest in dialect writing. Note the magazine stories in dialect.

2. Writing in different dialects in various localities. Dependence on dialect and overemphasis on this device. Note the writers of Southern mountaineer stories, other localities.
3. Discuss the work of Maurice Thompson and Harry Stillwell Edwards.
c. Search for the picturesque in different parts of America and popularity of the South in particular. The work of F. Hopkinson Smith, Thomas Nelson Page, George W. Cable.
1. Note the creation of stock characters, the impecunious, lovable Colonel, the devoted self-sacrificing Auntie and Uncle. Comment on Thomas Dixon's sensationalism in his use of the black man as villain.
2. The haze of romance which painted only the bright side of the bygone aristocracy.
3. The emphasis on background, local color. Different phases of plantation life depicted. Compare Dunbar's dialect poems.
d. Study in particular Thomas Nelson Page's *In Ole Virginia*, George W. Cable's *Old Creole Days*. Consider their value as records of a tradition and as a means of preserving details of slave life. Estimate the place of these books in American literature.

2. THE UNCLE REMUS TALES OF JOEL CHANDLER HARRIS

a. Discuss Harris' purpose in writing these tales, his theories concerning dialect transcription, and his ideas of the origin of the tales which he collected.
b. Compare the tales with fragments of African folk-lore.
c. Notice Harris' creation of a real character in Uncle Remus.
d. Discuss the picture of plantation life. Does Harris see the dark as well as the lighter side? Is his attitude that of a romanticist?
e. Read one of the tales and comment on the dialect, the folk-lore, and superstition embodied in it.
f. Estimate the value of the Uncle Remus stories as literature.

3. RECENT NEGRO FOLK-TALES

a. Gonzales' collections of tales from the Gullah Negro.
1. Discuss his use of dialect. Does its accuracy interfere with ease of reading? Compare the work of Mrs. Peterkin and Dr. Adams.
2. Compare his theories on folk-lore and dialect with those of Harris.
3. Discuss the Negro portrayed in these sketches. Compare Uncle Remus.
4. Read several of the stories aloud.

b. Dr. E. C. L. Adams' *Congaree Sketches*.
   1. Discuss the purpose of these sketches. Does Dr. Adams achieve more than a scientific transcription of folk-lore? Compare his dialogue with that of Gonzales. Note the characterization of both white and colored individuals.
   2. Note the poetry and imagination of some of the descriptions —"The Big Swamp of the Congaree," His Day Is Done," "The Falling Star," "Hell Fire."
   3. The homely wisdom and humor—"The Two Ducks," "The Hopkins Nigger," "Ole Sister in Hell," "Don't You Play Wid Married Wimmens," "If You Wants to Find Jesus."
   4. Superstition—Compare with the Uncle Remus tales "The Animal Court," "The Mule and the Ox," "The Little Old Man," "The Lake of the Dead."
   5. Irony and despair—"De Law Got Simon," "Ole Man Tooga's Chile," "Jonas," "Judge Fool Bird," "White Folks Is White Folks." Compare this indirect method with that of such propaganda writers as Walter White. Compare the attitude of the Negro in the *Congaree Sketches* with that shown in the first scene of *In Abraham's Bosom*.
   6. Estimate the worth of *Congaree Sketches*, the literary accomplishment of Dr. Adams.
c. Compare Odum's *Rainbow Round My Shoulder*.
d. Comment on the significance of the body of folk-lore to be found among the peasant type of Negro in the South, the need for its collection and preservation, its worth as material for literature.

REFERENCES

(Numerals refer to subjects)

Adams: *Congaree Sketches*. U. N. C. Press. (3)
Brawley: *The Negro in Literature and Art*. Duffield. (1, 2, 3)
Cable: *Old Creole Days*. Scribner. (1)
Cambridge History of American Literature. Putnam. (1, 2)
Cooper: *The Spy*. Houghton. (1)
Curtis-Burlin: *Songs and Tales from the Dark Continent*. Schirmer. (2)
Dixon: *The Clansman*. Doubleday. (1)
DuBois: *The Gift of Black Folk*. Stratford. (1, 2)
Edwards: *Aeneas Africanus*. Burke. (1)
        His Defense and Other Stories. Century. (1)
Gaines: *The Southern Plantation*. Columbia Univ. Press. (1, 2)
Gonzales: *The Black Border*. State Co. (3)
    The Captain. State Co. (3)
    La Guerre. State Co. (3)
    With Aesop Along the Black Border. State Co. (3)

Green: *The Field God* and *In Abraham's Bosom*. McBride. (3)
Harris: *Nights with Uncle Remus*. Houghton. (2)
        Uncle Remus and His Friends. Houghton. (2)
        Uncle Remus, His Songs and His Sayings. Appleton. (2)
Jessup: *Representative American Short Stories*. Allyn and Bacon. (1)
Library of Southern Literature. Martin and Hoyt. (1)
Locke: *The New Negro*, pp. 3-53, 231-249. Boni. (1, 2, 3)
Mikels: *Short Stories for High Schools*. Scribner. (1)
Moses: *The Literature of the South*. Crowell. (1, 2)
O'Brien: *The Advance of the American Short Story*. Dodd. (1, 2)
Odum: *Southern Pioneers*. U. N. C. Press. (3)
        Rainbow Round My Shoulder. Bobbs-Merrill. (3)
Page: *In Ole Virginia*. Scribner. (1)
Pattee: *A History of American Literature Since 1870*. Century. (1, 2)
        The Development of the American Short Story. Harper. (1, 2)
Poe: *The Gold Bug*. Putnam. (1)
Puckett: *Folk Beliefs of the Southern Negro*. U. N. C. Press. (3)
Ramsay: *Short Stories of America*. Houghton. (1)
Smith: *Colonel Carter of Cartersville*. Houghton. (1)
The South in the Building of the Nation. Southern Historical Pub. Soc. (1)
Stowe: *Uncle Tom's Cabin*. Dutton. (1)
Thompson: *Stories of the Cherokee Hills*. Houghton. (1)
Trent: *Southern Writers*. Macmillan. (1)
Twain: *Pudd'nhead Wilson*. Harper. (1)
Van Doren: *The American Novel*. Macmillan. (1)
White: *The Fire in the Flint*. Knopf.

MAGAZINES

American Mercury, 2: 190, June, 1924. (1, 2)
Dial, 66: 491-493, May 17, 1919. (2, 3)
Opportunity, 2: 327, November, 1924. (1, 2)
    4: 82-84, March, 1926.
    5: 195, July, 1927. (2, 3)
    6: 149 May, 1928.
Sewanee Review, January, 1916. (1)

    For bibliography of Negro folk-lore material, see Locke, *The New Negro*, pp. 438-443. For the vogue of dialect stories, consult the files of *The Atlantic Monthly, Harpers, Scribners*, and *The Century*, 1880-1900. Compare with contemporary use of dialect in the same magazines. Additional short story collections may be consulted, also additional works of the authors selected.

CHAPTER X

THE NEGRO BECOMES A CENTRAL CHARACTER

THE growing tendency towards realism, exemplified particularly by Hamlin Garland, Frank Norris, and Stephen Crane, caused American novelists in general to present their localities with impartial detail and to study their characters more deeply than did the local colorists. In the South, those who wrote of the past attempted to re-create a true picture. And the problem of race relations came to engage the best minds of both races; so that it was natural that there should arise a body of writing which is really propaganda, which paints the wrongs of the black man as the plantation romances painted his charm. Negro writers have used fiction as a vehicle to explain their ideas of advancement or to detail the wrongs of their people. The work of many white writers is valuable primarily as a measure of the new attitude toward the Negro.

Some of the more journalistic fiction writers and humorists have observed the foibles of the black man and caricatured him. Others have been appealed to by the color, variety, and vitality of Southern life and have rendered their impressions in artistic form.

Shands, Stribling, and Wood have been most successful in realizing the tragedy to white and black of the race conflict. Their books probe into the human significance of the struggle and present sincere and unbiased pictures of individual Negroes as the subjects of realistic novels.

Subjects for Study

1. A GENERAL SURVEY OF RECENT FICTION

a. Growth of realism.
   1. Writers of local color thought less of picturesqueness and more of the picture as a whole and its fidelity. Compare Cable's presentations of Creole life with those of Grace Elizabeth King and Kate Chopin.
   2. A group of young realists treated subjects which had been rejected by earlier writers. Note particularly Stephen Crane. His choice of subject in *The Monster*. Here the Negro is not an aid to background, nor is he treated as a problem. He is a simple individual.

b. Attempt to portray the past realistically, the historical novel.
  1. Note the work of Ellen Glasgow. Study the Negroes depicted. Are they emphasized for their picturesqueness or are they individualized? Discuss Miss Glasgow's studies of social problems in the new South.
  2. Discuss Mary Johnston's *The Slave Ship* and compare Evelyn Scott's *Migrations*. Note the attempts to portray even the worst side of slave life, without bias. Comment on the characterization in *Migrations*. Discuss the picture of the Civil War in James Boyd's *Marching On*.
c. The Negro caricatured in the humorous story.
  1. The work of Irvin S. Cobb, Octavus Roy Cohen, Robert McBlair. Note that Negroes are the central figures of these stories but they are always presented from the point of view of the white man. Compare humorous pieces from *Congaree Sketches*.
  2. What is the value of this farcical treatment which is intended to be exaggeration? Note other stock comedy figures such as the Irishman, the Yankee farmer, the Jew.
d. The Negro becomes the subject of serious realistic fiction.
  1. Summarize the efforts of a number of minor writers to present a fair picture of Negro life—George Madden Martin, Mary White Ovington, Paul Kester, Vara Majette, Dorothy Scarborough. (Note that the work of Shands, Wood, Stribling and that of a number of Negro writers will be considered in following papers.)
  2. The work of these writers is important historically for a new attitude toward the southern Negro. Note the number of southern women who have attempted a fair portrayal of conditions and a sympathetic study of Negro character.
e. The Negro in modern impressionistic fiction.
  1. Note Sherwood Anderson's use of minor figures to create a certain emotion, like the raucous careless laughter in *Dark Laughter*. Study Waldo Frank's *Holiday*. Note his impressionistic and poetic treatment of Negro background and figures, his emphasis on color and sound impressions.
  2. Carl Van Vechten's *Nigger Heaven*. Note the conflict between the impressionistic method of handling and the weight of exposition and propaganda. Compare Bodenheim's *Ninth Avenue*, also Claude McKay's *Home to Harlem*.
f. Summarize the general tendency to regard the Negro as a vital figure for artistic interpretation.

2. Negroes with a Thesis

a. The fiction of Paul Laurence Dunbar. Compare his dialect verse. Does his viewpoint differ from that of Page, Harris, and Cable? In his short stories note the simple presentation of plantation life.

b. Charles W. Chestnutt. Discuss his use of dialect and superstition, material gathered while teaching in the South. Note the problems which form the centers of his stories. Notice his treatment of the effect of Negro blood on one ostensibly white, a favorite theme since Mark Twain's *Pudd'nhead Wilson.* Comment on Chestnutt's characterization.

c. W. E. B. DuBois. Discuss his *The Quest of the Silver Fleece* and his *Dark Princess;* compare with his essays and sketches. Is he successful with the novel form? Is it merely a vehicle for propaganda?

d. Jessie Fauset's *There is Confusion.* Note the class of society from which the characters are drawn. Is she hampered by her efforts to prove the culture of Negroes? Is her point of view that of artist or thesis-writer? Do her characters live?

e. Walter White's novels.
  1. *The Fire in the Flint.* Note the experience of the author in investigating crimes against the black man in the South. What is his object in writing of them? Is it to expose conditions or to present a tragic picture of the human beings involved? Compare the work of Thomas Dixon. Which is more overdrawn and sensational? What is the value of *The Fire in the Flint* as literature? Compare with *In Abraham's Bosom.* Discuss the characterization. Note the dramatic irony of the events leading to the climax.
  2. *Flight.* Discuss the reality of the characters. Note the encumbrance of exposition, the failure to go below the surface effects of events. Compare other treatments of a Negro passing for white—Chestnutt and Wood.

f. Discuss the effect of these writers' consciousness of their race. What is the worth of their writings as literature?

3. Three Realistic Novels by White Writers

a. Hubert A. Shands' *White and Black.*
  1. Compare the point of view with that of *The Fire in Flint.* Which is the more sincere and complete? Does Shands try to solve a problem? Note that both races are affected by the tragedies of the situation.
  2. Are there real characters here? Note the dialect. Note that both white and black people are portrayed as human beings; each race has its good and bad individuals.

b. T. S. Stribling's *Birthright.*
  1. Comment on the main idea of the piece, the degenerating influence on an educated Negro of his racial inheritance and environment. Compare the theme with that of *In Abraham's Bosom.* Is Peter Siner's struggle truly deep and tragic? Discuss the ending of *Birthright.* Is it convincing and artistically true?

2. Discuss the character of Peter Siner, Cissie; the minor figures. Note the reality of dialogue when dialect is used. Discuss the white people presented, the effect upon them of their attitude towards the Negro.
  3. Notice that the action is moved, not by external forces like the enmity of the white race in *The Fire in the Flint*, but by forces inherent in the characters themselves. Does Stribling succeed in projecting his idea through his story?

c. Clement Wood's *Nigger*.
  1. In his attempt to present a realistic picture does Wood sacrifice a unity of plot and effect? Does he give a realistic impression? Note the variety of incident which is made a part of the story. Contrast the picturesque details used by the plantation writers to secure local color.
  2. Comment on the characterization. Note the vividness of most of the dialogue. Compare the return of Ophelia to her race with Peter Siner's absorption in it. Discuss the white people and Ophelia. Note that Wood is most successful when he adheres to the relations between individual Negroes. Compare the importance of the white man in this novel with that shown in *Birthright* and *White and Black*.

d. Estimate the value of these three novels.

REFERENCES

(Numerals refer to subjects)

Adams: *Congaree Sketches*. U. N. C. Press. (1)
Anderson: *Dark Laughter*. Boni and Liveright. (1)
Bodenheim: *Ninth Avenue*. Boni and Liveright. (1)
Boyd: *Marching On*. Scribner. (1)
Brawley: *The Negro in Literature and Art*. Duffield. (1, 2, 3)
Cable: *Old Creole Days*. Scribner. (1)
Cambridge History of American Literature. Putnam. (1, 2, 3)
Chestnutt: *The Conjure Woman*. Houghton. (2)
    The House Behind the Cedars. Houghton. (2)
Chopin: *Bayou Folk*. Houghton. (1)
Cobb: *J. Poindexter, Colored*. Doran. (1)
Cohen: *Bigger and Blacker*. Little. (1)
Crane: *The Monster and Other Stories*. Harper. (1)
DuBois: *The Dark Princess*. Harcourt. (2)
    The Gift of Black Folk. Stratford. (1, 2, 3)
    The Quest of the Silver Fleece. McClurg. (2)
Dunbar: *Folks from Dixie*. Dodd. (2)
Fauset: *There is Confusion*. Boni and Liveright. (2)
Frank: *Holiday*. Boni and Liveright. (1)
Gaines: *The Southern Plantation*. Columbia Univ. Press. (1, 2, 3)

Glasgow: *The Battle Ground.* Doubleday. (1)
   The Voice of the People. Doubleday. (1)
Green: *The Field God* and *In Abraham's Bosom.* McBride. (2, 3)
   Wide Fields. McBride.
Jessup: *Representative American Short Stories.* Allyn and Bacon. (1)
Johnston: *The Slave Ship.* Little. (1)
Kester: *His Own Country.* Bobbs-Merrill. (1)
King: *Monsieur Motte.* Doran. (1)
Library of Southern Literature. Martin and Hoyt. (1, 2)
Locke: *The New Negro.* Boni. (1, 2, 3)
McBlair: *Mister Fish Kelly.* Appleton. (1)
McKay: *Home to Harlem.* Harper. (1)
Majette: *White Blood.* Stratford. (1)
Martin: *Children of the Mist.* Appleton. (1)
O'Brien: *The Advance of the Amerian Short Story.* Dodd. (1, 2)
Ovington: *Hazel.* Crisis. (1)
   Portraits in Color. Viking. (2)
   The Shadow. Harcourt. (1)
Pattee: *Development of the American Short Story.* Harper. (1, 2)
   A History of American Literature Since 1870. Century. (1, 2)
Scarborough: *In the Land of Cotton.* Macmillan. (1)
Scott: *Migrations.* Boni. (1)
Shands: *White and Black.* Harcourt. (3)
The South in the Building of the Nation. Southern Hist. Pub. Soc. (1, 2)
Stribling: *Birthright.* Century. (3)
Trent: *Southern Writers.* Macmillan. (1)
Twain: *Pudd'nhead Wilson.* Harper. (2)
Van Doren: *The American Novel.* Macmillan. (1)
   Contemporary American Novelists. Macmillan. (1)
Van Vechten: *Nigger Heaven.* Knopf. (1)
White: *The Fire in the Flint.* Knopf. (2)
   Flight. Knopf.
Wood: *Nigger.* Dutton. (3)

MAGAZINES

Atlantic Monthly, 85: 699-701, 1900. (2)
Bookman, 55: 423, June, 1922. (3)
   60: 342, November, 1924. (2)
   50: 492, December, 1922. (3)
Crisis. (See index to files)
Dial, 60: 531-532, June 8, 1916. (1, 2, 3)
   72: 648, June, 1922. (3)
   73: 680, December, 1922. (3)
Fire, 1: 46, November, 1926. (1)
Independent, 108: 437-439, May 13, 1922. (3)

113: 202, September 27, 1924. (2)
116: 555, May 8, 1926. (2)
International Book Review, p. 555, June, 1924. (2)
Nation, 114: 498, April 26, 1922. (3)
New Republic, 30: 288-383, 1922. (3)
39: 192, July 9, 1924. (2)
Opportunity, 1: 31, February, 1923. (3)
2: 181, 342, 1924. (2)
4: 326, October, 1926. (2)
6: 151, May, 1928.
Sewanee Review, January, 1916. (1)

Some of the stories and novels listed here are out of print but may be found in the files of such magazines as *Scribners*. Chestnutt's works may be consulted there.

CHAPTER XI

TWO SOUTHERN NOVELISTS

In *Black April* and in *Porgy* the Negro has really come into his own in American fiction and assumed a place with all other characters who are flesh and blood, suffering, sinning, dying, and loving as human beings. For to Du Bose Heyward and Julia Peterkin there is no particular problem, only the wider, deeper struggle of existence. The Negro appeals to them because of his peculiar emotional endowments and because of the keenness of his hardships and the elemental force of his passions in the unsophisticated settings in which they have observed him. And so the aesthetic point of view is brought to bear, and we have the black man portrayed as a man, in no essential way different from his white brother in his hunger, love, and grief.

In their understanding of the Negro, these two authors have demonstrated, each in an individual manner, the ability of the white man to enter imaginatively into the particular racial experience of the black, and by sympathetic understanding of human impulses and emotions to portray that which is universal in their struggles. For it is an unproved and, perhaps, untenable theory that only the Negro writer can truly understand the heart of his people. Thus far when the colored writer has begun to probe below the surface of his characters he has become confused by his own problems and wrongs and inhibitions and has lost the detachment necessary to an artist who would create living characters. But Porgy and April and the accompanying people of their stories are real as the toil and dirt of the fields and the city slums. They move and breathe and entangle themselves in tragedy and by their reality prove that the white writers may know and understand the Negro.

1. JULIA PETERKIN

a. Experiences on an isolated plantation in South Carolina. Observation of the primitive and difficult lives of the Negroes who worked the land. The background for her work.

b. Her writing of poetry. She was advised to try fiction and published her first stories in *The Reviewer*. *Green Thursday* is her first book, a collection of stories having throughout a connecting thread of character and incident.

c. *Green Thursday.*
   1. The subject matter. Mrs. Peterkin has been criticized for including events and details of ugly brutality. Is she successful in forming them into a complete picture of the life she knows, or do they seem unnatural? Note that Mrs. Peterkin never seems to incorporate details for their value as local color, but for their place in a true presentation of the characters she knows.
   2. The style. Comment on the use of separate words and phrases in separate sentences. Does this broken rhythm accomplish its purpose? Does it give the impression of naturalness or does it mar smoothness? Is the author merely telling a story or does she go beneath the surface of events and attempt to interpret through mood and impression? Note the dialect and its rendering and compare the Gullah talk as transcribed by Gonzales.
   3. Characters. Discuss Mrs. Peterkin's method of relating the story through the thoughts of her people, a method intensified in *Black April*. Discuss the variety and reality of the portraits in *Green Thursday*. Contrast them with the romanticized Negroes of the "local color school." Which is the more true and complete interpretation?
d. Estimate the value of *Green Thursday* as literature.

2. "Black April"

a. The story. Comment on the looseness of the main thread of narrative. The character of April is the unifying element. Does this looseness make for greater sweep to the picture? Does the movement lag at times? Discuss the author's viewing of incidents through the minds of her characters. Is this always logical? Note the long explanations by these Negroes in their brooding over superstitions which would really seem to be a part of their accepted routine. Discuss the effectiveness of having April's fight with his son related through the eyes of a child.

Summarize the concluding events of the story and the death of April.

b. The characters. No white people appear in the books. Does this fact aid the author in her picture of this isolated Negro group? Note the vividness of the characterizations and the manner in which the incident arises from the interplay of character, the frictions caused by their natures and their primitive and human desires. Discuss the interpretation of April.

c. The background. Discuss the contention of W. E. B. DuBois that such a picture of Negro peasant existence is degrading to the race. Does Mrs. Peterkin accomplish an artistic interpretation of this hard and primitive life of the soil? Does her work partake of the universal drama of human struggle?

3. DuBose Heyward's "Porgy"

a. Life and works of Heyward. His poetry. Study in particular those which treat of South Carolina legend and background. Read *Jasbo Brown*. Briefly appraise *Angel*. Note the dramatization of *Porgy* by Dorothy Heyward.

b. *Porgy*.

1. Outline the story, noting the simplicity and directness of the narrative. Comment on the hurricane scene as a part of the action. Note the background—the homes of Charleston which have become the Negro slum section.
2. The characters. Heyward tells his story with detachment from his people, who do not interest him in their psychological complications but as actors in a colorful and touching drama of human conflict. Compare Mrs. Peterkin's approach to her presentation of the Negro. Discuss the white people in *Porgy*. Compare with those in *Mamba's Daughter*.
3. The style. Comment on the simplicity, clarity, and beauty of the writing. Note the poetry in some of the descriptive passages. Discuss the dialogue.
4. Estimate the value of *Porgy* in American literature.

c. *Mamba's Daughter* may be studied and compared with *Porgy*.

REFERENCES
(Numerals refer to subjects)

Heyward: *Mamba's Daughter*. Doran. (3)
    Porgy. Doran. (3)
Johnson: *Ebony and Topaz*, Nat. Urban League.
Peterkin: *Black April*. Bobbs-Merrill. (1, 2)
    Green Thursday, Knopf. (1, 2)

MAGAZINES

American Mercury, 6: 7-9, Sept. 1925 (Contains *Jasbo Brown*).
Bookman, 62: 333, November, 1925.
Crisis, 34: 129, June, 1927.
Independent, 115: 648, December 5, 1925.
International Book Review, p. 138, January, 1925.
Nation, 121: 711, December 16, 1925.
    121: 485-486, October 28, 1925.
New Republic, 45: 143, December 23, 1925.
New South, May, 1927.
New York Times, 5, March 6, 1927.
Opportunity, 2: 118, April, 1924.
Saturday Review of Literature, 781-783, May 15, 1926.
    3: 725, April 16, 1927.
Theatre Arts Monthly, 11: 903, December, 1927.

CHAPTER XII

NEGRO WRITERS OF FICTION

WITH the increase of cultural advantages the educated colored man is losing his inhibitions and gaining an artistic view of life. The number of Negro writers of fiction is continually growing, and these writers are obtaining an audience among prominent magazines and publishing houses. This fact might be ascribed to the current interest in the race, were it not for the increasing high average of this fiction and the emerging of two writers, in particular, to a high place in American contemporary letters. Jean Toomer and Eric Walrond in their work have proved that the Negro may be judged as an artist with no special consideration because of his race. For they have each a definite and original viewpoint and a particular style which causes their writing to be classed according to artistic approach and not according to subject matter. So Jean Toomer is an impressionist or an imagist and must be considered with that school of writers. That his work happens to be of and by a Negro forms a minor classification. The racial characteristics of his work are subordinated to his characteristics as an artist.

Both Toomer and Walrond would seem to place more importance upon style and method of presentation than upon the universal implications of the actions of their characters. In Walrond we find a preoccupation with the surfaces of the life he portrays; with Toomer the characters at times become abstractions, so bent is he upon creating the mood and expressing the spirit of his characters and their situations. Arthur Huff Fauset manifests the same tendency toward complete detachment from his people, and in this particular many of the younger Negro writers have swung to an extreme opposite to the viewpoint of the propaganda writers. Other more realistic writers have so far seemed rather journalistic than artistic in their approach to their material and their treatment of it. The decrease in race problem fiction, however, would lead to the expectation of an increase in aesthetic value and the emergence of a great and moving interpretation of the Negro by one of his own race.

1. Jean Toomer

a. Ancestry, early life, education, experience in Georgia as a schoolteacher.
b. His musical gifts, poetry. Publication of *Cane* in 1923. Residence at the Gurdjieff Institute in Fontainebleau, France, and resulting cessation of literary publication.
c. *Cane*.
   1. Influence of music and poetry are to be found in the striving after pattern and sound, often to the confusion of impression. Read *Carma* and comment on the rhythm and pattern there. Note that it begins and ends with poetry. Cite other examples of this method. Read aloud for the sound of the words and the sentence rhythm.
   2. The influence of Waldo Frank and Sherwood Anderson and of the extremists in modern literature. Formulate a definition of Toomer's aesthetic aims as exemplified in *Cane*. Compare his method in prose writing with that of his poetry, especially *Georgia Dusk* and *Song of the Son*.
   3. The material for *Cane*. Note the richness of the sense impressions, color, sound, and smell. The words used to convey these impressions are fresh and unhackneyed, often so homely as to partake of dialect. Comment on the folk-life which appeals to Toomer, his ability to see a strong and vital beauty in the sensuous, brutal, and degraded. Is he as successful with Washington as he is with Georgia life?
   4. Study particularly *Blood Burning Moon*. Is there any hint of the propagandist? Does Toomer achieve artistic detachment from problems affecting his race? Compare the closing scenes of *In Abraham's Bosom;* also Walter White's treatment of the lynching in *The Fire in the Flint*.
   5. Discuss *Kabnis*. Is Toomer successful with a sustained composition? Discuss *Kabnis* as narrative, as drama. Compare *Balo* from *Plays of Negro Life*.
d. Estimate Toomer's intellectual and artistic achievement.

2. Eric Walrond

a. Birth, education, public and journalistic work in Panama and in New York. Present identification with *Opportunity*.
b. Critical articles on racial and international relations. Publications in such journals as *The New Republic* and *Current History*. Recognition by national magazines. Inclusion in *The American Caravan* of a story of Harlem, "City Love."

c. *Tropic Death.*
1. The style. Discuss Walrond's successful reproductions of sense impressions—thirst, heat, terror, desire: to gain these effects, his use of vivid words and carefully measured sentences. Compare Mrs. Peterkin's writings. Note that Walrond describes almost entirely from the point of view of a spectator, while Mrs. Peterkin passes most of her impressions through the minds of her characters. Compare the work of Jean Toomer. Comment on the originality of Walrond's writing.
2. Language. Note the readily understandable transcription of a different dialect. Compare Gonzales' handling of the Gullah talk. Note the vivid language used to give an impression of the tropical background.
3. Characters. Notice the swift economical projection of the portraits, their variety and reality. Does Walrond probe beneath the surface of his characterizations?
4. Plot. Is the plot always clear? Does Walrond excel as a story-teller? What seems to come first with him—plot or atmosphere and impression? Discuss *Subjection.* Compare Paul Green's epilogue from *In the Valley.* Comment on the ironical ending of *Subjection* and *The Palm Porch.* Discuss the presence of this note of irony in the works of such members of the younger group as Cullen, Hughes, and Eulalie Spence.
5. Read from *Tropic Death* and *The Palm Porch.*

d. Give a critical estimate of the artistic worth of *Tropic Death,* its probable effect upon Negro writers and its place in American literature.

e. Review *Big Ditch.*

3. Negro Short Story Writers

a. The recognition of Negro writers by white editors of magazines. Note the inclusion of Negro work in such magazines as the *Atlantic Monthly* and in the prize collections of best short stories, O'Brien's and the O. Henry Memorial Award volumes.

b. Encouragement by Negro magazines through publication of stories and the prize competitions of *The Crisis* and *Opportunity.*

c. The work of Rudolph Fisher.
1. His early life, medical training, life in New York. The publication of his work in national magazines, prizes from competitions for Negroes.
2. His pictures of Harlem. Compare his approach with that of Carl Van Vechten in *Nigger Heaven.* Note his realistic descriptions, individualized characters, the humor, and often

ironic humor, of his tales. Note the story element and his skill at building plot through character. Do his stories show any O. Henry twists?
3. Read *The City of Refuge* and *Vestiges,* from *The New Negro,* and any other short stories from magazines. Sketch their plots and comment on their value. Do they show any particular depth of insight?
4. Discuss Fisher's novel. Is he more successful with the short story?
5. Compare McKay's *Home to Harlem.*

d. Study *Symphonesque,* by Arthur Huff Fauset. Compare the style with that of Toomer, Mrs. Peterkin, and Eric Walrond. Does this story partake more of fiction or of poetry? Note its imaginative quality, its rhythms and beauty of phrasing. Notice the inclusion of this story in the collections of O'Brien and the O. Henry Memorial Award, prizes from Negro magazines. Give a brief note on Arthur Huff Fauset, including a summary of his work in Negro folk-lore.

e. Summarize any other stories, from *The New Negro, Ebony and Topaz,* national Negro magazines. Discuss those which seem to you important.

REFERENCES
(Numerals refer to subjects)

The American Caravan (A story, "City Love"). Macaulay. (2)
Fisher: *The Walls of Jericho.* Knopf. (3)
Green: *The Field God* and *In Abraham's Bosom.* McBride.
    In the Valley. French. (2)
    Wide Fields. McBride.
Johnson, C. S.: *Ebony and Topaz.* Nat. Urban League.
Locke: *The New Negro.* Boni. (3)
Locke and Gregory: *Plays of Negro Life.* Harper. (1)
McKay: *Home to Harlem.* Harper. (3)
O'Brien: *The Best Short Stories of 1923—.* Small. (3)
O. Henry Memorial Award Prize Stories of 1923—. Doubleday. (3)
Ovington: *Portraits in Color.* Viking. (1, 2, 3)
Peterkin: *Green Thursday.* Knopf. (2)
Rosenfeld: *Men Seen.* Dial. (1)
Toomer: *Cane.* Boni and Liveright. (1)
Van Vechten: *Nigger Heaven.* Knopf. (3)
Walrond: *Tropic Death.* Boni and Liveright. (2)
    Big Ditch. Boni. (2)
White: *The Fire in the Flint.* Knopf. (1)

MAGAZINES

American Mercury, 11: 393-398, August, 1927.
Atlantic Monthly, 135: 652, 1925.
    139: 37, 1927.
    140: 183, August, 1927.
Books, New York Herald Tribune. p. 9, December 5, 1926.
Crisis, (consult files, especially numbers containing prize stories.)
Current History Magazine, 17: 786-788, February, 1923.
    19: 121-123, October, 1925.
Double Dealer, January 6, 1926.
Independent, 114: 8-11, 1925.
    117: 260-262, 1926.
Literary Review, 333: December 8, 1923.
McClure's, August, 1927.
New Republic, 32: 244-246, 1922.
    35: 200-201, 1923.
    48: 332, 1926.
    37: 126, 1923.
New South, 1: May, 1927.
Opportunity, 1: 374, December, 1923.
    3: 262-263, September, 1925.
    4: 178, June, 1926.
    (Consult files, especially numbers containing prize stories.)
Survey, 51: (Supplement) 190, November 1, 1923.
    57: 159, 1926.
World Tomorrow, 7: 96, March, 1924.

PART IV. CRITICISM

CHAPTER XIII

THE OLD AND THE NEW IN RACE RELATIONS

Out of the welter of Reconstruction days, when the South was at the beginning of its industrial development, the Negro found in Booker T. Washington a leader whose conservative program advocated the raising of his race by industrial education and by the gradual development of economic independence. Being a man of forceful personality, a practical thinker, and an orator of ability, he was looked to by both races for a safe solution of adjustment problems. His speeches and his writings on social questions are important to any study of race relations. The simplicity and clarity of his autobiography rank it as literature.

But his ideas were not entirely adequate. They did not satisfy the slowly increasing minority of educated individuals in his race who felt that their rights were being jeopardized for the sake of friendly relations with the white South, and the spiritual and mental progress of the race sacrificed for the comfort of the laboring masses. This element in the race found in W. E. B. DuBois a brilliant and impetuous leader, one sensitive to wrong and injustice, a leader with courage to cry out bitterly against them. His significance is more than a social one. He has the emotional gifts and the eloquence of a poet. His essays and other prose writings are important in the literature of his race and of America.

1. Booker T. Washington

a. Ancestry, early life, and education at Hampton Institute. The aims of this institution.

b. The building of Tuskegee. Some of the difficulties encountered. The spread of the program for industrial education.

c. The speeches which made him a recognized leader of his race. Discuss his ability in oratory and comment briefly on other Negro orators, such as Douglass.

d. Study carefully his speech at the Cotton Exposition in Atlanta in 1895. The program he laid down here has been called "The Atlanta Compromise." Why? Comment upon the results of this speech, the attitude of the white South and the objections of intellectuals in the Negro race.

e. Note how Washington reflected the political and economic ideas of his period. Discuss his statesmanship.
f. Review *Up from Slavery.* Estimate its place in American biography. What is the artistic value of Washington's writing?

2. THE LEADERSHIP OF W. E. B. DuBois

a. Ancestry, early life, education.
b. Doctor's thesis. *The Suppression of the Slave Trade,* sociological study and investigation.
c. Teacher and leader. Atlanta University, 1896-1910. Establishment of Atlanta University Studies of Negro Problems. Niagara Movement, 1905.
d. The National Association for the Advancement of Colored People. Du Bois' work with this organization.
e. Editorship of *The Crisis.* The general policy of this magazine. Examples of Dr. DuBois' editorials. Articles in national magazines of white editorship.
f. Unequivocal leadership in times of crisis, such as the Atlanta riot, and labor conflicts.
g. International problems. Founding of the Pan-African Congress, 1919.
h. Compare the work of DuBois with that of Washington.

3. THE ESSAYS OF DU BOIS

a. A rapid survey of his books, exclusive of the essays.
  1. *The Negro in the South.* Compare his style with that of Washington's papers, included in this volume.
  2. *John Brown.* (In American Crisis Biographies.)
  3. *The Quest of the Silver Fleece,* and *Dark Princess,* novels.
  4. *Star of Ethiopia,* a pageant.
  5. *The Negro.*
  6. *The Gift of Black Folk.*
b. *The Souls of Black Folk* and *Darkwater.*
  1. Consciousness of the wrongs of his race gives his essays tragic depth and poignancy, the strength of powerful convictions and devotion to a cause.
  2. Does this lead to over-bitterness? Is his artistic intent marred by propaganda?
  3. The style of these essays. Note the poetical suggestiveness, vividness of others. Study *The Sorrow Songs* and *The Veil.* Compare *A Litany of Atlanta* with the prose work and give reasons for his greater success as an essayist.
c. Estimate Dr. DuBois' contribution to American literature.

REFERENCES

(Numerals refer to subjects)

Adams: *Congaree Sketches.* (Introduction.) U. N. C. Press. (1, 2)
Brawley: *The Negro in Literature and Art.* Duffield. (1, 2, 3)
    A Short History of the American Negro. Macmillan. (1, 2, 3)
    A Social History of the American Negro. Macmillan. (1, 2, 3)
Cambridge History of American Literature. Putnam (1, 2)
Detweiler: *The Negro Press in the United States.* U. of Chicago. (2)
DuBois: *Dark Water.* Harcourt. (3)
    The Gift of Black Folk. Stratford. (2, 3)
    John Brown. Jacobs. (2, 3)
    The Negro. Holt. (2, 3)
    The Souls of Black Folk. McClurg. (2, 3)
    The Suppression of the African Slave Trade. Harvard Univ. Press. (2, 3)
Fauset: *For Freedom.* Franklin. (1, 2)
Johnson: *The Book of American Negro Poetry.* Harcourt. (3)
Journal of Negro History. Association for Study of Negro Life. (1)
Kerlin: *The Voice of the Negro.* Dutton. (2)
Locke: *The New Negro.* Boni. (1, 2, 3)
Mims: *The Advancing South.* Doubleday. (1, 2)
Modern Eloquence. vol 9. Shuman. (1)
Moses: *The Literature of the South.* Crowell. (1, 2)
Odum: *Southern Pioneers.* U. N. C. Press. (1)
Ovington: *Portraits in Color.* Viking. (2, 3)
Peabody: *Education for Life.* Doubleday. (1)
South in the Building of the Nation. Southern Hist. Pub. Soc. (1, 2)
Thrasher: *Tuskegee.* Small. (1)
Washington: *Up from Slavery.* Doubleday. (1)
    My Larger Education. Doubleday. (1)
    The Story of the Negro. Doubleday. (1)
Washington and Du Bois: *The Negro in the South.* Jacobs. (1)
Woodson: *The Negro in our History.* Associated Publishers. (1, 2)
    Negro Orators and Their Orations. Associated Publishers. (1, 2)

MAGAZINES

American Mercury, 3: 179-185, October, 1924.
Atlantic Monthly, 115: 707-714, May, 1915. (2, 3)
Century, 105: 538-548, February, 1923. (2, 3)
Crisis. (See index of files.)
Current History, 21: 690-700, February, 1925. (2)
    22: 559, July, 1925.
Dial, 61: 525-527, December 14, 1916. (1)
Forum, 73: 178-188, February, 1925. (2)

Independent, 102: 235, May 15, 1920. (3)
Nation, 101: 588-589, November 18, 1915. (1)
        110: 726, 757-758, 1920. (3)
        111: 350-352, September, 1920. (2, 3)
        116: 539-541, May 9, 1923. (2, 3)
        119: 675-676, December 17, 1924. (2, 3)
        120: 63-67, January 21, 1925. (2, 3)
New Republic, 5: 60-61, November 20, 1915. (1)
        21: 338-341, February 18, 1920. (2, 3)
        22: 189, April 7, 1920. (3)
        33: 138-141, January 3, 1923. (2)
        37: 142-145, January 2, 1924. (2)
        44: 326-329, November 18, 1925. (2)
Nineteenth Century, 88: 909-913, November, 1920. (2, 3)
Opportunity, 6: 102, April, 1927.
Outlook, 111: November 24, 1915. (1)
        112: 410-411, February 23, 1916. (1)
        114: 101-104, September 13, 1916. (1)
        115: 23-24, January 3, 1917. (1)
Southern Workman, January, 1916. (See index of files)
Survey, 53: 655-657, March 7, 1925. (2)

CHAPTER XIV

"THE NEGRO"

VARIOUS forces have worked to bring forth the new spirit in the race. Education, economic freedom, growth of class distinctions, social and cultural advantages—all these and many more have wrought upon the race as a whole to bring about a new group psychology. The New Negro has sloughed off his protective covering of self-praise, over-sensitiveness, exaggerated accusation of his oppressor. He has repudiated any special allowances, the appeals on which he has, in the past, been tempted to lean. He stands upon a certain pride in the history and the gifts of his race, but he looks beyond the limits of his particular group to a consciousness of national and international identity. Even in the most sensational journalistic protests against discrimination we find the editor sounding a new note of confident demand for rights. The Negro newspaper of today stresses most strongly the idea of race-coöperation, but in all matters not pertaining to the defense of the race the press is apt to be conservative, even reactionary. In this it resembles the majority of white journals, which tend to reflect, rather than determine, the attitude of its readers.

The wider education of the Negro has given its intellectual leaders an audience within the race so that they are no longer mere spokesmen to the whites. At the same time the new white man begins to realize, on one hand, the importance of the racial contribution in American life and literature, and on the other the identity of the Negro's thought with that of any other American writer or thinker. The "Negro Renaissance" has focused attention on everything that is racial, but since high attainment produced this interest, it cannot fail to continue beyond the special stimulation of a passing fad.

1. THE NEGRO NEWSPAPER

a. Reasons for news agencies separate from white newspapers. Number and distribution of present newspapers. Agencies and syndicates for obtaining news.
b. The Negro press in the development of the race. *Frederick Douglass' Paper* and others. Growth of Negro literacy led to increase of demand for news.

c. The Negro press during the World War and the labor stress following.
d. Detailed study of leading Negro newspapers.
Make-up, amount of advertising and syndicated "fillers," types of news, local news, international affairs, Negro institutions, sports, literature and art, music, the theatre.
e. Editorial policies. Participation in local and national politics. General tenor of race relations. Discuss Dr. Locke's assertion that the Negro is "radical on race matters, conservative on others."
f. Critical study of the editorials of leading papers.
(NOTE: The following may be studied: Baltimore *Afro-American*, Norfolk *Journal and Guide*, Savannah *Tribune*, Atlanta *Independent*, Washington (D. C.) *Tribune*, St. Louis *Argus*, Philadelphia *Tribune*, Pittsburgh *Courier*, Kansas City *Call*, Chicago papers—*Defender, Whip, Bee*. New York papers— *New York Age, Amsterdam News*.

2. TWO NEGRO MAGAZINES

a. The Crisis.
1. Study the make-up of this magazine, fiction, poetry, illustrations, articles. Estimate the service it is doing to Negro artists. Note the prize contests and other encouragements.
2. Editorial policy. Are race journalism and race propaganda overemphasized? Note the authority of experience, scientific investigation, and thought behind many of the articles.
3. Any change in the magazine since its establishment in 1910?
4. Note the staff of *The Crisis* and the association supporting it; note the race leaders who are contributors, the movements which this paper has fostered. What is its weight in political and international affairs?

b. Opportunity.
1. Observe the make-up of the magazine. Compare with *The Crisis* as regards format.
2. The general tone of editorial and critical articles, lack of bitterness and racial sensitiveness, note of race pride balanced with consciousness of existence as an integral part of American life. How does this paper exemplify the spirit of the "New Negro," as defined by Dr. Locke?
3. Encouragement of literature and art. Study particularly the columns of Countee Cullen and Gwendolyn Bennett. Is there genuine criticism here? Note the prize contests, publication of stories and poetry, attention to American literature in general, without narrow confinement to race.
4. "The Negro Renaissance." How is this new spirit shown in the editorials on cultural and educational matters? In those dealing with labor problems, international affairs, etc.?

5. Charles S. Johnson, the editor. Note his work in various fields. Read selected editorials.
6. Review *Ebony and Topaz*.

3. "THE NEW NEGRO"

a. The development of this volume from the Harlem Number of the *Survey Graphic*, March, 1925. Note the inclusion in the magazine of a larger number of special sociological studies.
b. The purpose of *The New Negro*, as stated in Dr. Locke's Foreword.
c. The significance to Negroes, critically, creatively and in other ways.
d. Summarize the contributions here in various departments, the articles of literary and general social criticism, the specialized treatments of education, economics, labor problems, international relations, race cultures. Note that most of the Negro contributors have reputations outside of their own race.
e. Study the articles by Alain Locke, particularly the paper on "The New Negro."
f. Response to this volume by the reading public, particularly the white element.

REFERENCES
(Numerals refer to subjects)

Detweiler: *The Negro Press in the United States*. U. of Chicago. (2)
Fauset: *For Freedom*. Franklin. (1, 2)
Johnson, C. S.: *Ebony and Topaz*. Nat. Urban League. (1, 2, 3)
Kerlin: *The Voice of the Negro*. Dutton. (1, 2, 3)
Locke: *The New Negro*. Boni. (1, 2, 3)
Mims: *The Advancing South*. Doubleday. (1 2, 3)
Ovington: *Portraits in Color*. Viking. (1, 2, 3)

MAGAZINES

American Mercury, 7: 354-356, February, 1926. (3)
    8: 207-215, June, 1926. (1)
Carolina Magazine, May, 1927. (3)
Century, 111: 635-637, March, 1926. (3)
Crisis. (See files).
New Republic, 46: 371, May 12, 1926. (3)
Opportunity, 1: 29, February, 1923. (1, 2)
    2: 365, December, 1924. (1, 2)
    3: 50, 162-187, 1925. (1, 2)
    4: 54-55, 74, 80, 374-375, 1926. (2, 3)
    4: 374-375, 80, 1926. (2, 3)
    5: 227, 358-363, 1927. (2, 3)
Saturday Review of Literature, 2: 572, February 20, 1926. (3)
Survey Graphic, 53: March 1, 1925. (3)
NOTE—For the first discussion obtain current issues of newspapers named, also any local newspapers.

SPECIAL REFERENCE BIBLIOGRAPHY

Adams, E. C. L.: *Congaree Sketches*. University of North Carolina Press. 1927. $2.00. (2, 4, 9, 10, 13)

American Caravan, The. The Macaulay Co. 1927. $5.00. (9, 12)

Anderson, Sherwood: *Dark Laughter*. Boni and Liveright. 1925. $2.50. (10)

Ballanta, Nicholas G. J.: (See Taylor, A.) (1)

Bechhofer, C. E.: *The Literary Renaissance in America*. London. Heinnemann. 1923. $1.50. (7)

Bodenheim, Maxwell: *Ninth Avenue*. Boni and Liveright. 1927. $2.00. (10)

Boucicault, Dion: *The Octoroon*. (See Quinn, *Representative American Plays*.) (6)

Boyd, James: *Marching On*. Scribner. 1927. $2.50. (10)

Boynton, Percy H.: *Some Contemporary Americans*. University of Chicago Press. 1924. $2.00. (7)

Braithwaite, William Stanley: *Anthologies of Magazine Verse, 1913—*. Brimmer Co. 1913—. $2.00. (2, 3)

The House of Falling Leaves. Luce. 1908. $1.00. (3)

Lyrics of Life and Love. Turner. 1904. $1.00. (3)

Brawley, Benjamin: *The Negro in Literature and Art*. Duffield. 1926. $1.50. (1, 2, 3, 5, 6, 7, 9, 10, 13)

A Short History of the American Negro. Macmillan. 1919. $2.00. (13)

A Social History of the American Negro. Macmillan. 1921. $4.00. (13)

Cable, G. W.: *Old Creole Days*. Scribner. 1892. $2.00. (9, 10)

Cambridge History of American Literature. 14 vols. Putnam. 1921. $3.50 each. (9, 10, 13)

Chestnutt, C. W.: *The Conjure Woman*. Houghton. 1899. $2.00. (10)

The House Behind the Cedars. Houghton. 1900. (10)

Chopin, Kate: *Bayou Folk*. Houghton. 1904. (10)

Clark, Barrett: *Eugene O'Neill*. McBride. 1926. $1.00. (7)

A Study of the Modern Drama. Appleton. 1925. $4.50. (7)

The Writings of Paul Green. McBride. (1, 2, 3)

Cobb, Irvin S.: *J. Poindexter, Colored*. Doran. 1922. $2.00. (10)

Cohen, Octavus Roy: *Bigger and Blacker*. Little. 1925. $2.00. (10)

Cooper, J. Fenimore: *The Spy*. Houghton. 1911. $1.00. (9)

Crane, Stephen: *The Monster and Other Stories*. Harper. 1889. $1.25. (10)

Cullen, Countee: *Caroling Dusk*, an Anthology. Harper. 1927. $2.50. (1, 2, 3, 4)

Color. Harper. 1925. $2.00. (4)

Copper Sun. Harper. 1927. $2.00. (4)

Curtis-Burlin, Natalie: *The Hampton Series of Negro Folk-Songs.* Schirmer. 1918. $.50. (1)
    Songs and Tales from the Dark Continent. Schirmer. 1920. $4.00. (1, 9)
Detweiler, Frederick G.: *The Negro Press in the United States.* University of Chicago Press. 1923. $3.00. (2, 5, 13, 14)
Dickinson, T. H.: *Playwrights of the New American Theatre.* Macmillan. 1925. $2.50. (7)
Dixon, Thomas: *The Clansman.* Doubleday. 1905. $1.50. (9)
Du Bois, W. E. B.: *Dark Princess.* Harcourt. 1928. $2.00. (10, 13)
    Dark Water. Harcourt. 1921. $2.25. (13)
    The Gift of Black Folk. Stratford. 1924. $2.00. (1, 2, 3, 5, 6, 7, 9, 10, 13)
    John Brown. Jacobs. 1909. $1.25. (13)
    The Negro. Holt. 1915. $1.00. (13)
    The Quest of the Silver Fleece. McClurg. 1911. $1.35. (10)
    The Souls of Black Folk. McClurg. 1903. $2.00. (1, 13)
    The Suppression of the African Slave Trade. Harvard University Press. 1896. $2.00. (13)
Dunbar, Paul Laurence: *Complete Poems.* Dodd, Mead. 1925. $2.50. (1)
    Folks from Dixie. Dodd, Mead. 1898. $1.50. (10)
Edwards, Harry Stillwell: *Aeneas Africanus.* Burke. 1922. $.50. (9)
    His Defense and Other Stories. Century. 1899. $1.75. (9)
Fauset, Arthur Huff: *For Freedom.* Franklin Pub. Co. 1927. $2.00. (13, 14)
Fauset, Jessie Redmon: *There is Confusion.* Boni and Liveright. 1924. $1.00. (10)
Fisher, Rudolph: *The Walls of Jericho.* Knopf. 1928. $2.50. (12)
Frank, Waldo: *Holiday.* Boni and Liveright. 1923. $2.00. (10)
Gaines, Francis Pendleton: *The Southern Plantation.* Columbia University Press. 1924. $2.50. (1, 2, 5, 6, 9, 10)
Glasgow, Ellen: *The Battle Ground.* Doubleday. 1902. $2.00. (10)
    The Voice of the People. Doubleday. 1902. $2.00. (10)
Gonzales, Ambrose E.: *The Black Border.* State Co. 1922. $3.00. (9)
    The Captain. State Co. 1924. $3.00. (9)
    La Guerre. State Co. 1924. $2.00. (9)
    With Aesop Along the Black Border. State Co. 1924. $2.00. (9)
Green, Paul: *The Field God* and *In Abraham's Bosom.* McBride. 1927. $2.00. (8, 9, 10, 12)
    In Aunt Mahaly's Cabin. French. 1925. $.50. (8)
    In the Valley. French. 1927. $2.50. (8, 12)
    Lonesome Road. McBride. 1926. $2.00. (8)
    The Lord's Will. Holt. 1925. $2.00. (8)
    The Man Who Died at Twelve O'Clock. French. 1925. $.50. (8)
    The No 'Count Boy. (See *In the Valley* and *Lonesome Road* and *Theatre Arts Monthly.* Nov., 1924.) (8)

Supper for the Dead. (See *American Caravan.*) (8)
Wide Fields. McBride. 1928. $2.50. (9, 12)
Grimke, Angelina W.: *Rachel.* Cornhill Co. 1920. $1.25. (5)
Hamilton, Clayton: *Conversations on Contemporary Drama.* Macmillan. 1924. $2.00. (7)
Handy, W. C.: *Blues.* A. & C. Boni. 1926. $3.50. (1, 4, 5)
Harris, Joel Chandler: *Nights with Uncle Remus.* Houghton. 1893. $2.25. (9)
    Uncle Remus and His Friends. Houghton. 1892. $2.25. (9)
    Uncle Remus, His Songs and His Sayings. Appleton. 1916. $2.00. (1, 2, 9)
Heyward, DuBose: *Mamba's Daughter.* Doran. (announced.) (11)
    Porgy. Doran. 1925. $2.00. (11)
Heyward, Dorothy and DuBose: *Porgy*, dramatized. Doubleday. 1928. $1.00. (11)
Heyward, DuBose, and Allen, Hervey: *Carolina Chansons.* Macmillan. 1922.
Hughes, Langston: *Fine Clothes to the Jew.* Knopf. 1927. $2.00. (4)
    The Weary Blues. Knopf. 1927. $2.00. (4)
Jessup, Alexander: *Representative American Short Stories.* Allyn and Bacon. 1923. $4.00. (9, 10)
Johnson, Charles S. (ed.): *Ebony and Topaz.* Nat. Urban League. 1927. (2, 4, 10, 11, 12, 14)
Johnson, Georgia Douglas: *Plumes.* French. 1927. $.30. (5)
Johnson, James Weldon: *The Autobiography of an Ex-Coloured Man.* Knopf. (Blue-Jade Library.) 1927. $3.00. (3)
    The Book of American Negro Poetry. Harcourt. 1922. $1.75. (1, 2, 3, 4, 5, 13)
    Fifty Years and Other Poems. Viking. 1928. (3)
    God's Trombones. Viking. 1927. $2.50. (3)
Johnson, J. W. and J. R.: *The Book of American Negro Spirituals.* Viking. 1925. $3.50. (1, 3)
    The Second Book of American Negro Spirituals. Viking. 1926. $3.50. (1, 3)
Johnston, Mary: *The Slave Ship.* Little. 1924. $2.00. (10)
Journal of Negro History. Association for the Study of Negro Life and History. 1916—. (13)
Kennedy, R. Emmet: *Black Cameos.* A. & C. Boni. 1924. $2.50. (1)
    Mellows. A. & C. Boni. 1925. $5.00. (1)
Kerlin, Robert J.: *Negro Poets and Their Poems.* Associated Publishers. 1922. $2.50. (1, 2, 13)
    The Voice of the Negro. Dutton. 1920. $2.50. (13, 14)
Kester, Paul: *His Own Country.* Bobbs-Merrill. 1917. $1.50. (10)
King, Grace Elizabeth: *Monsieur Motte.* Doran. 1907. $1.25. (10)
Krehbiel, Henry Edward: *Afro-American Folk-Songs.* Schirmer. 1914. $2.00. (1)

Leonard, William Ellery: *The Lynching Bee*. Viking. 1920. $1.50. (2)
Lewis, B. Roland: *Contemporary One-Act Plays*. School Edition. Scribner. 1922. $1.50. (8)
Library of Southern Literature. Martin and Hoyt. 1907. (9, 10)
Lindsay, Vachel: *Collected Poems*. Macmillan. 1925. $3.50. (3, 4)
Locke, Alain: *Four Negro Poets*. Simon and Schuster. 1926. $.25. (2, 3, 4)
    The New Negro. A. & C. Boni. 1925. $5.00. (1, 2, 3, 4, 5, 6, 7, 9, 10, 12, 13, 14)
Locke, A. and Gregory, M.: *Plays of Negro Life*. Harper. 1927. $5.00. (5, 6, 7, 8, 12)
McBlair, Robert: *Mister Fish Kelly*. Appleton. 1924. $2.00. (10)
McKay, Claude: *Harlem Shadows*. Harcourt. 1922. $1.35. (3)
    Home to Harlem. Harper. 1927. $2.50. (3)
McNeill, John Charles: *Lyrics from Cotton Land*. Stone Publishing Co. 1907. $1.50. (1, 2)
Majette, Vara A.: *White Blood*. Stratford. 1924. $2.00. (10)
Martin, George Madden: *Children of the Mist*. Appleton. 1920. $1.75. (10)
    The Lion's Mouth. Appleton. 1920. $.50. (6)
Millay, Edna St. Vincent: *Renascence*. Mitchell Kennerley. 1921. $1.50. (4)
Mikels, Rosa M.: *Short Stories for High Schools*. Scribner. 1915. $1.00. (9)
Mims, Edwin: *The Advancing South*. Doubleday. 1926. $3.00. (13, 14)
Modern Eloquence. vol. IX. Shuman. 1903. (13)
Monroe, Harriet, and Henderson, Alice C.: *The New Poetry*. Macmillan. 1924. $2.50. (2, 3, 4)
Moses, Montrose J.: *The Literature of the South*. Crowell. 1910. $4.50. (9, 10, 13)
    Representative American Dramas. Little. 1925. $4.50. (7)
    Representative Plays by American Dramatists. vol. II. Dutton. 1925. $3.00. (6)
Niles, John J.: *Singing Soldiers*. Scribner. 1927. $3.00. (1, 4)
O'Brien, Edward J.: *The Advance of the American Short Story*. Dodd, Mead. 1923. $2.00. (9, 10)
    The Best Short Stories of 1923—. Small. 1924—. $2.00. (12)
Odum, Howard W. (ed.): *Southern Pioneers*. University of North Carolina Press. 1925. $2.00. (9, 13)
    Rainbow Round My Shoulder. Bobbs-Merrill. 1928. $3.00. (9)
Odum, H. W., and Johnson, G. B.: *The Negro and His Songs*. University of North Carolina Press. 1925. $3.00. (1)
    Negro Workaday Songs. University of North Carolina Press. 1926. $3.00. (1, 5)
O. Henry Memorial Award Prize Stories of 1925—. Doubleday. 1926—. (11)
O'Neill, Eugene: *All God's Chillun Got Wings* and *Welded*. Boni and Liveright. 1924. $2.50. (7)
    Complete Works. vol. II. Boni and Liveright. 1924. $2.50. (7)
    Emperor Jones. Appleton. 1921. $.50. (7)

(Also Boni and Liveright. 1925. $2.50)
The Dreamy Kid. (See *Theatre Arts Magazine.* January, 1920)
Also vol. II, *Complete Works.* Also volume with *Emperor Jones,
Gold,* and *The First Man.*)
Welded. Boni and Liveright. (See *All God's Chillun.*) (7)

Ovington, Mary White: *Hazel.* Crisis Publishing Co. 1913. $1.00. (10)
    Portraits in Color. Viking. 1927. $2.00. (3, 4, 5, 12, 13, 14)
    The Shadow. Harcourt. 1920. $1.75. (10)
Page, Thomas Nelson: *In Ole Virginia.* Scribner. 1922. $1.75. (1, 2, 9)
Pattee, Fred Lewis: *Development of the American Short Story.* Harper. 1923. $2.50. (9, 10)
    A History of American Literature Since 1870. Century. 1915. $2.50. (9, 10)
Peabody, Francis G.: *Education for Life.* Doubleday. 1915. $2.50. (13)
Peterkin, Julia: *Black April.* Bobbs-Merrill. 1927. $2.50 (11)
    Green Thursday, Knopf. 1924. $2.50. (11, 12)
Poe, Edgar Allan: *The Gold Bug.* Putnam. $.75. (9)
Puckett, Newbell Niles: *Folk Beliefs of the Southern Negro.* University of North Carolina Press. 1926. $5.00. (9)
Quinn, Arthur Hobson: *Contemporary American Plays.* Scribner. 1923. $2.00. (7)
    Representative American Plays. Century. 1917. $2.75. (6)
Ramsay, Robert L.: *Short Stories of America.* Houghton. 1921. $1.50. (9)
Rosenfeld, Paul: *Men Seen.* Dial Press. 1925. $2.50. (12)
Rowland, Mabel: *Bert Williams, Son of Laughter.* English Crafters. 1923.
(5)
Sayler, Oliver M.: *Our American Theatre.* Brentano's. 1923. $4.00. (7)
Scarborough Dorothy: *In the Land of Cotton.* Macmillan. 1923. $1.50. (10)
    On the Trail of Negro Folk Songs. Harvard University Press. 1925. $3.50. (1)
Scott, Evelyn: *Migrations.* A. & C. Boni. 1927. $2.50. (10)
Seldes, Gilbert: *The Seven Lively Arts.* Harper. 1924. $4.00. (5)
Sergeant, Elizabeth S.: *Fire Under the Andes.* Knopf. 1927. $4.00. (5, 7)
Shands, Hubert A.: *White and Black.* Harcourt. 1922. $1.90. (10)
Shay, Frank: *Twenty Contemporary One-Act Plays—American.* Appleton. $3.75.
    Fifty More Contemporary One-Act Plays. Appleton. 1928. $5.00.
(5)
Sheldon, Edward: *The Nigger.* Macmillan. 1910. $1.25. (6)
Smith, Alice M.: *Short Plays by Representative Authors.* Macmillan. 1920. $1.80. (6)
Smith, F. Hopkinson: *Colonel Carter of Cartersville.* Houghton. 1901. $2.00.
(9)
The South in the Building of the Nation. Southern Historical Society. 1909.
(9, 10, 13)

Spence, Eulalie: *The Fool's Errand*. French. 1927. $.50. (5)
Stowe, Harriet Beecher: *Uncle Tom's Cabin*. Dutton. 1900. $.35 and $.70. (9)
　　Uncle Tom's Cabin (Dramatization). French. (6)
Stribling, T. S.: *Birthright*. Century. 1922. $2.00. (10)
Talley, Thomas W.: *Negro Folk Rhymes*. Macmillan. 1922. $2.25. (1)
Taylor, A., and Ballanta, N. G. J.: *St. Helena Spirituals*. Schirmer. 1925.
Thompson Maurice: *Stories of the Cherokee Hills*. Houghton. 1898. $1.50.
　　　　(9)
Thrasher, Max Bennet: *Tuskegee*. Small. 1901. (13)
Toomer, Jean: *Cane*. Boni and Liveright. 1927. $2.00. (2, 5, 11, 12)
Torrence, Ridgely: *Granny Maumee, The Rider of Dreams, Simon the Cyrenian*. Macmillan. 1917. $1.75. (6)
Trent, W. P.: *Southern Writers*. Macmillan. 1905. $2.40. (9, 10)
Twain, Mark: *Pudd'nhead Wilson*. Harper. 1899. $2.25. (9, 10)
Untermeyer, Louis: *American Poetry Since 1900*. Holt. 1923. $3.50. (2, 3, 4)
Van Doren, Carl: *The American Novel*. Macmillan. 1921. $2.00. (9, 10)
　　Contemporary American Novelists. Macmillan. 1922. $1.50. (10)
Van Vechten, Carl: *Nigger Heaven*. Knopf. 1926. $2.50. (6, 10, 12)
Walrond, Eric: *Big Ditch*. Boni and Liveright. 1928. $2.50. (12)
　　Tropic Death. Boni and Liveright. 1926. $2.50. (12)
Washington, Booker T.: *Up From Slavery*. Doubleday. 1910. $2.00. (13)
　　My Larger Education. Doubleday. 1911. $1.50. (13)
　　The Story of the Negro. Doubleday. 1909. $3.00. (13)
Washington, B. T., and Du Bois, W. E. B.: *The Negro in the South*. Jacobs, 1907. $1.00. (13).
White, Newman I.: *American Negro Folk-Songs*. Harvard University Press. 1928. $5.00. (1)
White, Newman I., and Jackson, W. C.: *An Anthology of Verse by American Negroes*. Duke University Press. 1924. $2.00. (1, 2, 3)
White, Walter F.: *The Fire in the Flint*. Knopf. 1924. $2.50. (9, 10, 12)
　　Flight. Knopf. 1926. $2.50. (10)
Wood, Clement: *Nigger*. Dutton. 1922. $2.00. (10)
　　Poets of America. Dutton. 1925. $3.00. (2, 3, 4)
Woodson, Carter G.: *The Negro in Our History*. Associated Publishers. 1922. $3.15. (13)
　　Negro Orators and Their Orations. Associated Publishers. 1925. $5.00. (13)
Work, F. J.: *Some American Negro Folk Songs*. Boston. 1909. (1)
Work, J. W.: *Folk Songs of the American Negro*. Fisk University Press. 1915. $1.10. (1)

MAGAZINE DIRECTORY

Below is a list of the magazines and newspapers referred to in this program. Back numbers of the magazines and perhaps the newspapers may be obtained from either F. W. Faxon Co., 83 Francis Street, Boston, Mass., or from H. W. Wilson Co., 958 University Ave., New York City, if they cannot be obtained from the publishers, but at a higher price. Many libraries have these publications on file where they may be consulted. Numerals refer to chapters in which they are mentioned.

American Magazine: The Crowell Pub. Co., Springfield, Ohio.
    Yearly, $2.50; single copies, $.25.
        70: 600-604, Sept. 1910. (5)
        85: 33-35, Jan. 1918. (5)

American Mercury: Alfred A. Knopf, Publishers, 730 Fifth Ave., N .Y. C., or Federal and 19th Streets, Camden, New Jersey.
    Yearly, $5.00; single copies, $.50.
        1: 110, Jan. 1924. (7)
        1: 243-4, Feb. 1924. (5, 6)
        2: 113-5, May, 1924. (5, 7)
        2: 190, June, 1924. (9)
        2: 371-2, July, 1924. (5)
        2: 371-372, July, 1924. (3)
        3: 179, Oct. 1924. (13)
        6: 7-9, Sept. 1925.
        7: 354-356, Feb. 1926. (14)
        9: 500-2, Dec. 1926. (5, 7)
        8: 207-215, June, 1926. (1)
        10: 394, April, 1927. (3)
        11: 395-8, Aug. 1927. (5, 12)

Arts and Decoration: Arts and Decoration Publishing Co., Inc., 578 Madison Ave., N. Y. C.
    Yearly, $6.00; single copies, $.50.
        April, 1927. (8)

Atlantic Monthly: Atlantic Monthly Company, Rumford Building, Concord, New Hampshire, or 8 Arlington Street, Boston, Mass.
    Yearly, $4.00; single copies, $.40.
        20: 608, Nov. 1867. (5)
        24: 71, July, 1869. (5)
        85: 699-701, May, 1900. (10)
        115: 707-714, May, 1915. (13)
        135. 652, May, 1925. (12)

139: 37, Jan. 1927. (12)
140: 183, Aug. 1927. (12)

Baltimore Evening Sun, Baltimore, Maryland.
Nov. 16, 1926. (8)
May 1, 1927. (8)

Black Opals: Care of Allan R. Freelon, 2220 Catherine Street, Philadelphia.
Any issue. (2)

Bookman: Bookman Publishing Co., Inc., 452 Fifth Ave., N. Y. C.
Yearly, $5.00; single copies, $.50.
50: 492, Dec. 1922. (10)
55: 423, June, 1922. (10)
55: 531, July, 1922. (3)
60: 342, Nov. 1924. (10)
62: 333, Nov. 1925. (11)
62: 503, Dec. 1925. (4)
63: 122, March, 1926. (1)

Boston Evening Transcript: Boston, Mass.
May 5, 1927. (8)

Carolina Magazine: Chapel Hill, N. C.
May, 1927. (2, 4, 5, 14)
May, 1928. (2)

Century: The Century Co., 353 Fourth Ave., N. Y. C., or Concord, N. H.
Yearly, $5.00; single copies, $.50.
105: 539-548, Feb. 1923. (13)
111: 635-637, March, 1926. (14)
112: 510, Aug. 1926. (8)
113: 682, April, 1927. (3)

Commonweal: Calvert Pub. Corp., Grand Central Terminal, 25 Vanderbilt Ave., N. Y. C.
Yearly, $10.00. Published weekly.

Crisis: Nat. Asso. for the Advancement of Colored People. 69 Fifth Ave., N. Y. C.
Yearly, $3.00; single copies, $.25
Aug. 1916, p. 169. (5)
April, 1919. (1)
Nov. 1919. (5, 6)
March, 1927, 34: 12. (8)
April, 1927. (5)
June, 1927, 34: 129. (11)
34: 85-103, 229, 248, 1927. (5)

Current History: New York Times Co., Times Square, N. Y. C.
Yearly, $3.00; single copies $.25.
17: 786-788, Feb. 1923. (12)
19: 121-123, Oct. 1925. (12)

21: 690-700, Feb. 1925. (13)
22: 559, July, 1925. (13)

Dial: Dial Publishing Co., 152 West 13th Street, or 19th and Federal Streets, Camden, New Jersey.
Yearly, $5.00; single copies, $.50.
49: 522, Dec. 16, 1910. (6)
60: 531-532, June 8, 1916. (10)
61: 525-527, Dec. 14, 1916. (13)
63: 529, Nov. 22, 1917. (6)
66: 491-493, May 17, 1919. (9, 10)
72: 648, June, 1922. (10)
73: 680, Dec. 1922. (9, 10)

Doubledealer: Doubledealer Publishing Co., 204 Baronne Street, New Orleans, La. (Suspended publication.)
Yearly, $2.50; single copies, $.25.
January 6, 1926. (12)

Drama: Drama Corporation, 55 West 42nd Street, N. Y. C., or 404 N. Wesley Ave., Mount Morris, Illinois.
Yearly, $3.00; single copies. $.50.
16: 54, Nov. 1925.
16: 224, March, 1925. (5)
17: 136, Feb. 1927. (8)
17: 233, May, 1927. (8)

Fire: 314 West 138th Street, N. Y. C.
Yearly $4.00; single copies, $1.00.
Any issue. (2)
1: 46, Nov. 1926. (10)

Forum: Forum Publishing Co., 441 Lexington Ave., N. Y. C., or 10 Ferry Street, Concord, New Hampshire.
Yearly, $4.00; single copies $.35.
73: 174-188, Feb. 1925. (13)

Freeman: Ceased publication.
7: March 21, 1923. (7)

Harper: Harper and Bros., Pub., 49 East 33rd Street, N. Y. C., or 10 Ferry Street, Concord, New Hampshire.
Yearly, $4.00; single copies, $.35.
Jan. and June, 1889. (5)

Independent: Independent Publications, 10 Ferry St., Concord, New Hampshire, or 10 Arlington St., Boston, Mass.
Yearly, $5.00; single copies, $.15.
92: 63, Oct. 6, 1917. (6)
102: 235, May 15, 1920. (13)
108: 437-439, May 13, 1922. (10)
109: 54, Aug. 5, 1922. (3)

113: 202, Sept. 27, 1924. (10)
114: 8-11, Jan. 3, 1925. (12)
115: 539, Nov. 7, 1925. (4)
115: 648, Dec. 5, 1925. (11)
116: 555, May 8, 1926. (10)
117: 260-62, Sept. 4, 1926. (12)

International Book Review: Ceased publication.
June, 1924, p. 555. (10)
Jan. 1925, p. 138. (11)

Journal of American Folk-Lore: American Folk-Lore Society, Care of G. E. Stechert, 31-35 East 10th St., N. Y. C.
Yearly, $4.00; single copies, $1.50.
35: 223, 1922. (1)

Literary Digest: Funk & Wagnalls Co., 354-360 Fourth Avenue, N. Y. C.
Yearly, $4.00; single copies, $.10.
June 10, 1911. (5)
48: 1114, May 9, 1914. (5, 6)
72: 28-29, March 25, 1922.
May 28, 1927, p. 21. (8)

Munsey: Ceased publication.
May, 1908. (5)

McCall's Magazine: McCall Co., Inc., 236 W. 37th St., N. Y. C.
Yearly, $1.00; single copies, $.10.
54: 27, Sept. 1927. (8)

McClure's Magazine: International Publications, Inc., 119 W. 40th St., New York City.
Yearly, $3.00; single copies, $.25.
August, 1927. (8)

Nation: Nation Inc., 20 Vesey St., New York City.
Yearly, $5.00; single copies, $.15.
91: 272, Sept. 22, 1910. (6)
101: 588-589, Nov. 19, 1915. (13)
110: 726, May 29, 1920. (13)
110: 756-757, June 5, 1920. (13)
111: 350-352, Sept. 1920. (13)
114: 349, March 22, 1922. (7)
114: 498, April 26, 1922. (10)
114: 694, June 7, 1922. (3)
116: 539-541, May 9, 1923. (13)
116: 605-606, May 23, 1923. (5)
118: 664, June 4, 1924. (5, 7)
119: 675-676, Dec. 17, 1924. (13)
120: 63-67, Jan. 1925. (13)
121: 485-486, Oct. 28, 1925. (8, 11)

121: 711, Dec. 16, 1925. (11)
121: 763, Dec. 30, 1925. (4)
122: 692-694, June 23, 1926. (1, 2)
124: 403, April 13, 1927. (2)
124: 510-511, May 4, 1927. (8)

New Republic: New Republic, Inc., 421 West 21st St., New York City.
Yearly, $5.00; single copies, $.15.
5: 60-61, Nov. 20, 1915. (13)
10: 325, April 14, 1917. (6)
21: 338, 341, Feb. 18, 1920. (13)
22: 189, April 7, 1920. (13)
28: 350, Nov. 16, 1921. (5)
30: 288, May 3, 1922. (9)
30: 383, May 24, 1922. (9)
32: 244-246, Nov. 1, 1922. (12)
33: 138-141, Jan. 3, 1922. (13)
35: 200-201, July 18, 1922. (12)
37: 126, Dec. 26, 1923. (12)
37: 142-145, Jan. 2, 1924. (13)
39: 192, July 9, 1924. (10)
44: 326-329, Nov. 8, 1925. (13)
45: 143, Dec. 23, 1925. (11)
46: 40-44, March 3, 1926. (5)
46: 179, March 31, 1926. (4)
46: 197-198, April 7, 1926. (7)
46: 371-2, May 12, 1926. (14)
48: 332, Nov. 10, 1926. (12)
50: 46, March 2, 1927. (8)
51: 76-77, June 8, 1927. (4)
51: 260, July 27, 1927. (8)
52: Nov. 16, 1927. (7)

New South: New South Publishing Company, Chattanooga, Tenn.
Yearly, $3.00; single copies. $.25.
May, 1927. (11, 12)

New York Evening Post Literary Review: 75 West St., New York City.
May 7, 1927. (8)
Dec. 8, 1923, p. 333. (12)

New York Herald Tribune: 225 West 40th St., New York City.
Dec. 31, 1926. (8)

New York Times Book Review: Times Square, New York City.
Aug. 29, 1926. (8)
Jan. 9, 1927. (8)
March 6, 1927. (11)
May 8, 1927. (8)
April 15, 1928.

New York World Book Review: 53-63 Park Row, New York City.
April 17, 1927.

Nineteenth Century: Leonard Scott Publication Co., 249 West 13th Street, New York City.
Yearly, $7.00; single copies, $.75.
54: 27, Sept. 1927. (8)

Opportunity: National Urban League, 17 Madison Avenue, N. Y. C.
Yearly $1.00; single copies, $.15.
1: 29, Feb. 1923. (14)
1: 30, Feb. 1923. (6, 10)
1: 292, Oct. 1923. (1)
1: 374, Dec. 1923. (12)
2: 113, April, 1924. (7, 11)
2: 221, July, 1924. (7)
2: 327, Nov. 1924. (9)
2: 360, Dec. 1924. (7, 14)
3: 51, Feb. 1925. (14)
3: 63, Feb. 1925. (6)
3: 121, April, 1925. (8)
3: 181, June, 1925. (1, 2)
3: 162-187, June, 1925. (2, 14)
3: 282, Sept. 1925. (8)
3: 330-336, Nov. 1925. (1, 5, 7)
4: 14, Jan. 1926. (4)
4: 54-55, Feb. 1926. (14)
4: 72-3, Feb. 1926. (4)
4: 74, Feb. 1926. (14)
4: 82-84, March, 1926. (9)
4: April, 1926. (6)
4: 146-160, May, 1926. (4)
4: 158, May, 1926. (1, 2)
4: 178, June, 1926. (12)
4: June, 1926. (2)
4: July, 1926. (2)
4: 257: Aug. 1926. (4)
4: 294, Sept. 1926. (8)
4: 374-376, Dec. 1926. (8, 14)
4: 381, Dec. 1926. (4)
5: 54, Feb. 1927. (6, 8)
5: 53, Feb. 1927. (5)
5: 86, March, 1927. (5, 8)
5: 84-86, April, 1927. (4)
5: 108-110, April, 1927. (2, 4)
5: 195, July, 1927. (9)
5: 270-271, September, 1927. (2, 3, 4)

BIBLIOGRAPHIES AND DIRECTORIES

    5: 227, Aug. 1927. (14)
    5: 358-363, Dec. 1927. (2, 3)
    5: 200, July, 1927. (5)
    6: 102, April, 1928. (2, 3)
    6: 90, 122, 153, 166, 180, 214. 1928. (5)

Outlook: Outlook Co., 120 East 16th St., New York City.
    Yearly, $5.00; single copies, 15c.
        111: p. Nov. 24, 1915.
        112: 410-411, Feb. 23, 1916.
        114: 101-104, Sept. 13, 1916.
        115: 23-24, Jan. 3, 1917.

Palms: Guadalajara, Mexico.
    Yearly, $1.50; single copies, 25c.
        October, 1926. (2, 3, 4)

Poetry: 232 East Erie St., Chicago, Illinois.
    Yearly, $3.00; single copies, 25c.
        28: 50-53, April, 1926. (4)

Raleigh News and Observer: Raleigh, N. C.
    Jan. 9, 1927. (8)
    March 20, 1927. (8)

Reviewer: Ceased publication.
    All issues for 1925.

Review of Reviews, American: 55 Fifth Avenue, New York City.
    Yearly, $4.00; single copies, 35c.
        56: 444, Oct. 1917. (6)

Saturday Review of Literature: Saturday Review Co., Inc., 25 West 45th St., New York City.
    Yearly $3.50; single copies, 10c.
        2: 572, Feb. 20, 1926. (14)
        781-783, May 15, 1926. (8, 14)
        3: 312, April 9, 1927. (4)
        3: 725, April 16, 1927. (11)
        3: 940-941, July 2, 1927. (8)

Scribner's Magazine: Charles Scribner's Sons, 597 Fifth Avenue, New York City.
    Yearly, $4:00; single copies, 35c.
        June, 1915.

Sewanee Review: University of the South, Sewanee, Tenn.
    Yearly, $4.00; single copies, 75c.
        Jan. 1916. (9, 10)

Southern Workman: Hampton Normal and Agricultural Institute, Hampton, Virginia.
    Yearly, $1.00; single copies, 10c.
        238-245, April, 1912. (1)

172-176, April, 1918. (1)
243-247, May 1918. (1)
563-565, Dec. 1925. (1)
371, Dec. 1926. (3)
177, April, 1927. (2, 4)

Survey: Survey Associates, Inc., 112 East 19th St., New York City.
Yearly, $5.00; single copies 25c.
51: 190, Nov. 1, 1923. (12)
53: March 1, 1925. (14)
53: 655-657, March 7, 1925. (13)
57: 169, Nov. 1, 1926. (12)

Theatre Arts Monthly, Inc.: (formerly *Theatre Arts Magazine*) 119 West 57th St., New York City.
Yearly $4.00; single copies, 50c.
4: 41, Jan. 1920 (*Dreamy Kid*).
5: 29, Jan. 1921 (*Emperor Jones*). (7)
8: 487, July, 1924. (7)
10: 112-120, Feb. 1926. (5, 6)
10: 701-706, Oct. 1926. (5, 6, 7)
11: 282-293, April, 1927. (5)
11: 903, Dec. 1927. (7, 11)

Travel: Robert M. McBride & Co., 7 West 16th St., New York City.
Yearly, $4.00; single copies, 35c.
June, 1927.

The World Tomorrow: Fellowship Press, Inc., 104 E. 9th St., New York City.
Yearly, $1.00; single copies, 10c.
7: 96, March, 1924. (12)

A PARTIAL LIST OF LITERATURE BY AND ABOUT THE NEGRO SINCE 1900

I. Poetry

NOTE: Because of the fact that many of the titles of this bibliography were privately published, it has been impossible to secure the dates and publishers.

Adams, Wellington: *Lyrics of Humble Birth.* Washington, D. C., 1914.
Allen, Hervey: (See Heyward, DuBose).
Allen, J. Mord: *Rhymes, Tales, and Rhymed Tales.* Topeka, Kan., 1906.
Bailey, William Edgar: *The Firstling.* 1914.
Battle, Mrs. Effie T.: *Gleamings From Dixie.* Okolona, Miss., 1916.
Beadle, S. A.: *Lyrics of the Underworld.* Jackson, Miss., 1912.
Bell, James Madison: *Poetical Works.* Wynkoop, Hallenbeck, Crawford Co., Lansing, Mich., 1901.

Blades, William C.: *Negro Poems and Melodies.* Badger, Boston, 1921.
Braithwaite, William Stanley: *Anthology of Magazine Verse.* Brimmer, Boston. 1913—.
    Lyrics of Life and Love. Small, Boston. 1904.
    The House of Falling Leaves. Luce, Boston. 1908.
    Sandy Star and Willie Gee (announced). Boston, Mass.
Brawley, Benjamin G.: *The Problem and Other Poems.* Atlanta, 1905.
    The Desire of the Moth for the Star. Atlanta, 1906.
    The Dawn and Other Poems. Washington. 1911.
    The Seven Sleepers of Ephesus. Atlanta. 1917.
    A Toast of Love and Death. Atlanta. 1902.
Burleigh, Louise Alston: *Echoes from the Southland.*
Carmichael, Waverly Turner: *From the Heart of a Folk.* Cornhill, Boston, 1918.
Clifford, Carrie Williams: *The Widening Light.* Walter Reid Co., Boston, 1922.
Cloud, Virginia Woodward: *Candlelight.* Norman Remington, Baltimore, 1924.
    From an Old Garden. Norman Remington, Baltimore, 1924.
Coleman, J. H.: *Poems.* John P. Morton Co., Louisville, Ky., 1918.
Conner, Charles H.: *The Enchanted Valley.* Philadelphia, 1917.
Corbett, Maurice Nathaniel: *The Harp of Ethiopia.* Nashville, 1914.
Corrothers, James David: *Selected Poems.* 1907.
    The Dream and the Song. 1916.
Cotter, Joseph S., Sr.: *A White Song and a Black One.* Louisville, Ky., 1909
    Life's Dawn and Dusk. (announced).
Cotter, Joseph S., Jr.: *The Band of Gideon and Other Lyrics.* Cornhill Co., Boston, 1918.
    Out of the Shadows. (announced).
Cullen, Countee: *Caroling Dusk,* an Anthology. Harper, New York, 1927.
    Color. Harper, New York, 1925.
    Copper Sun. Harper, New York, 1927.
Dancer, W. E.: *Facts, Fun and Fiction.* Jacksonville, Fla.
    Today and Yistidy. Tuskegee, Ala., 1914.
Dandridge, Ray G.: *The Poet and Other Poems.* Cincinnati, 1920.
    Penciled Poems. Cincinnati, 1917.
Dett, R. Nathaniel: *The Album of a Heart.*
Dinkins, Charles R.: *Lyrics of Love, Sacred and Secular.* Columbia, S. C., 1904.
Dunbar, Paul Laurence: *Complete Poems.* Dodd, Mead, New York, 1925.
Dunbar-Nelson, Alice Moore: *A Dunbar Speaker and Entertainer.* J. L. Nichols Co., Naperville, Ill., 1920.
Fleming, Sarah Lee Brown: *Clouds and Sunshine.* Cornhill, Boston, 1920.
Ford, Robert E.: *Brown Chapel,* A Story in Verse. 1905.
Fortune, Timothy Thomas: *Dreams of Life.* New York, 1905.

Fulton, David B.: *Abraham Lincoln.* Brooklyn, 1909.
Hammon, Jupiter: *Selections and Bibliography of.* Edited by Oscar Wegelin. Heartman, New York, 1915.
Harris, Leon R.: *The Steelmaker and Other War Poems.* 1918.
Hawkins, Walter Everette: *Chords and Discords.* Badger, Boston, 1920.
Heyward, DuBose: *Skylines and Horizons.* Macmillan. 1924.
Heyward, DuBose and Allen, Hervey: *Carolina Chansons.* Macmillan. 1922.
Hill, Leslie P.: *The Wings of Oppression.* The Stratford Co., Boston, 1921.
    Toussaint L'Ouverture. Christopher Publishing House, Boston. 1928.
Holloway, John Wesley: *From the Desert.* Neale Publishing Co., New York, 1919.
Hughes, Langston: *Weary Blues.* Knopf. New York, 1926.
    Fine Clothes to the Jew. Knopf, New York, 1927.
Jackson, W. C. (See White, Newman I.)
Jamison, Roscoe C.: *Negro Soldiers and Other Poems.* William F. McNeill, South St. Joseph, Mo.
Johnson, Adolphus: *The Silver Chord.* Philadelphia, 1915.
Johnson, Charles Bertram: *Wind Whisperings.* 1900.
    The Mantle of Dunbar and Other Poems. 1918.
    Songs of My People. Cornhill, Boston. 1918.
Johnson, Georgia Douglas: *Bronze.* Brimmer, Boston, 1922.
    The Heart of a Woman. Cornhill, Boston, 1918.
    An Autumn Love Cycle (announced).
Johnson, Fenton: *A Little Dreaming.* Chicago, 1913.
    Songs of the Soil. New York, 1916.
Johnson, James Weldon: *The Book of American Negro Poetry.* Harcourt, Brace, New York, 1922.
    Fifty Years and Other Poems. (New Edition) The Viking Press, New York, 1928.
    God's Trombones. The Viking Press, New York, 1927.
Jones, Edward Smythe: *The Sylvan Cabin and Other Verse.* Sherman, French, Boston, 1911.
Jones, Joshua Henry, Jr.: *Poems of the Four Seas.* Cornhill, Boston, 1921.
    The Heart of the World. Stratford, Boston, 1919.
Kerlin, Robert T.: *Negro Poets and Their Poems.* Associated Publishers, Washington, D. C., 1923.
Leonard, William Ellery: *The Lynching Bee.* Huebsch, New York, 1920.
Lindsay, Vachel: *Collected Poems.* Macmillan, New York, 1925.
Locke, Alain: *Four Negro Poets* (Toomer, McKay, Cullen, Hughes). Simon and Schuster, New York, 1926.
McClellan, G. M.: *The Path of Dreams.* John P. Morton and Co., Louisville, Ky., 1916.
McKay, Claude: *Cornstab Ballads.* London, 1912.
    Harlem Shadows. Harcourt Brace, New York, 1922.

Songs of Jamaica, Kingston, Jamaica, 1912.
Spring in New Hampshire. London, 1921.
McGirt, James E.: *Some Simple Songs*. Philadelphia, 1901.
For Your Sweet Sake. Winston Co., Philadelphia, 1909.
McNeill, John Charles: *Lyrics From Cottonland*. Stone Publishing Co., Charlotte, N. C., 1907.
Margetson, George Reginald: *England in the West Indies*. 1906.
Ethiopia's Flight. 1907.
Songs of Life. Sherman, French, Boston, 1910.
The Fledgling Bard and the Poetry Society. Badger, Boston, 1916.
Means, Sterling M.: *The Deserted Cabin and Other Poems*. A. B. Caldwell, Atlanta, 1915.
The German War Lord and the British Lion. The Pauley Co., Indianapolis, Ind., 1918.
The Black Devils and Other Poems. The Pentecostal Pub. Co., Louisville, Ky., 1919.
Monroe and Henderson: *The New Poetry*. Macmillan, New York, 1924.
Moore, William, H. A.: *Dusk Songs*.
Nailor, Alexander J.: *Divinely Inspired Message*. Oakland, California, 1922.
Oxley, L. G.: *Souls of Colored Poets*, an Anthology. Boston (announced).
Ray, H. Cordelia: *Poems*. The Grafton Press, New York, 1910.
Russell, Irwin: *Christmas Night in the Quarters and Other Poems*. The Century Co., New York, 1917.
Shackelford, Otis M.: *Seeking the Best*. Kansas City, Mo., 1911.
Shackelford, Theodore Henry: *Mammy's Cracklin' Bread and Other Poems*. Reading, Pa., 1900.
Shackelford, William H.: *Poems*. Nashville, Tenn., 1907.
Temple, George H.: *The Epic of Columbus' Bell*. Reading, Pa., 1900.
Thompson, Clara Ann: *Songs from the Wayside*. Rossmoyne, Ohio, 1908.
Thompson, Priscilla Jane: *Ethiope Lays*. Rossmoyne, Ohio, 1900.
Gleanings of Quiet Hours. Rossmoyne, Ohio, 1907.
Toomey, Richard, E. S.: *Thoughts for True Americans*. Washington, D. C., 1901.
Underhill, Irving W.: *Daddy's Love and Other Poems*. Philadelphia.
Watkins, Lucian B.: *Voices of Solitude*. Donohue and Co., Chicago, 1907.
Whispering Winds.
Weeden, Howard: *Songs of the Old South*. Doubleday, Page, Garden City, N. Y., 1900.
Wheatley, Phyllis: *Poems and Letters*. (Edited by Charles F. Heartmann.) New York, 1915.
Wheeler, B. F.: *Cullings from Zion's Poets*. Mobile, Ala., 1907.
White, Newman I. (and Jackson, W. C.): *An Anthology of Verse by American Negroes*. Duke University Press, Durham, N. C., 1924.
Whitman, A. A.: *An Idyll of the South*. New York, 1901.

Wilds, Myra Viola: *Thoughts of Idle Hours*. Nashville, Tenn., 1915.
Williams, Edward W.: *The Views and Meditations of John Brown*. Washington, D. C., 1908.

II. Fiction

Adams, Clayton: *Ethiopia the Land of Promise*. The Cosmoplitan Press, New York, 1917.
Adams, E. C. L.: *Congaree Sketches*. The University of North Carolina Press, Chapel Hill, N. C., 1927.
    Nigger to Nigger. Scribner's, New York. (announced.)
American Caravan, The: The Macaulay Co., New York, 1927.
Anderson, Sherwood: *Dark Laughter*. Boni and Liveright, New York, 1925.
Anonymous: *Bayette: a South African Novel*. Cape Town, Africa, 1925.
Ashby, William M.: *Redder Blood*. Neale Publishing Co., New York, 1916.
"Asterisk": *Gone Native*. Constable and Co., London.
Azevedo, Aluizio: *A Brazilian Tenement*. McBride, New York, 1926.
Benefield, Barry: *Short Turns*. Century Co., New York, 1926.
Bodenheim, Maxwell: *Ninth Avenue*. Boni and Liveright, New York, 1927.
Bradford, Roark: *Ol' Man Adam an' his Chillun*. Harper, New York, 1928.
Bryant, H. E. C.: *Tar Heel Tales*. Stone Publishing Co., Charlotte, N. C., 1910.
Cable, G. W.: *Old Creole Days*. Scribner's, New York. 1907.
    (See *Works*.)
Chestnutt, Charles W.: *The House Behind the Cedars*. 1900.
    The Marrow of Tradition. 1901.
    The Colonel's Dream. Doubleday, Page and Co., Garden City, N. Y., 1905.
    (See *Works*.)
Chopin, Kate: *Bayou Folk*. Houghton Mifflin, New York, 1904.
Cobb, Irvin S.: *J. Poindexter, Colored*. Doran, New York, 1922.
Cocke, Sarah: *Old Mammy Tales from Dixie Land*. Dutton, New York, 1911.
Cohen, Octavus Roy: *Polished Ebony*. Dodd, Mead, New York, 1919.
    Come Seven. Dodd, Mead, 1920.
    Highly Colored. Dodd, Mead, 1921.
    Assorted Chocolates. Dodd, Mead, 1922.
    Dark Days and Black Knights. Dodd, Mead, 1923.
    Bigger and Blacker. Little, Brown, Boston, 1925.
    Black and Blue. Little, Brown, 1926.
Conrad, Joseph: *The Nigger of the Narcissus*. Doubleday, Page, Garden City, N. Y., 1914.
Corrothers, James D.: *The Black Cat*. Funk and Wagnalls, New York, 1902.
Cotter, Joseph S.: *Negro Tales*. The Cosmopolitan Press, New York, 1912.
Cozart, W. F.: *The Chosen People*. Christopher Press, Boston, 1924.
Crane, Stephen: *The Monster and Other Stories*. Harper, New York, 1900.
    Works. Knopf. 1925-1926.

Davis, J. Frank: *Almanzar*. Henry Holt, New York, 1918.
Dix, Dorothy: *Mirandy*. Hearst's International Library, New York, 1914.
   Mirandy Exhorts. Penn Publishing Co., Philadelphia. 1922.
Dixon, Thomas: *The Clansman*. Doubleday, Page, Garden City, N. Y., 1905.
   The Fall of a Nation. Donohue, Chicago, 1918.
   The Leopard's Spots. Doubleday, Page, Garden City, N. Y., 1902.
Dreer, Herman: *The Immediate Jewel of His Soul*. The St. Louis Argus Publishing Co., 1919.
DuBois, W. E. B.: *The Quest of the Silver Fleece*. McClurg, Chicago, 1911.
   Dark Princess. Harcourt, Brace, New York, 1928.
Dunbar, Paul Laurence: *The Love of Landry*. Dodd, Mead, New York, 1900.
   The Sport of the Gods. Dodd, Mead, 1901.
   The Fanatics. Dodd, Mead, 1901.
   The Strength of Gideon and Other Stories. Dodd, Mead, 1902.
   Heart of Happy Hollow. Dodd, Mead, 1904.
Durham, John S.: *Diane, Priestess of Hayti*. Lippincott, Philadelphia, 1902.
Edwards, Harry Stillwell: *Aeneas Africanus*. J. W. Burke and Co., Macon, Ga., 1920.
   Two Runaways and Other Stories. Century, New York, 1906.
Fauset, Jessie Redmon: *There is Confusion*. Boni and Liveright, New York, 1924.
Firbank, Ronald: *Sorrow in Sunlight*.
   Prancing Nigger. Brentano's, New York, 1924.
Fisher, Rudolph: *The Walls of Jericho*. Knopf, New York, 1928.
Fleming, Sarah Lee Brown: *Hope's Highway*. Neale Publishing Co., New York, 1917.
Frank, Doctor (pseudonym): *Negrolana*. The Christopher Publishing Co., Boston, 1924.
Frank, Waldo: *Holiday*. Boni and Liveright, New York, 1923.
Frazer, W. H.: *The Possumist and Other Stories*. Murrill, Charlotte, N. C., 1924.
Garnett, David: *The Sailor's Return*. Knopf, New York, 1925.
Gilmore, F. Grant: *The Problem*. The Neale Publishing Co., New York, 1915.
Glasgow, Ellen: *The Voice of the People*. Doubleday, Page, Garden City, N. Y., 1902.
   The Battle Ground. Doubleday, Page, Garden City, 1902.
   (See *Works*.)
Glenn, Isa: *Southern Charm*. Knopf, New York, 1928.
Gonzales, Ambrose E.: *The Black Border*. The State Co., Columbia, S. C., 1922.
   The Captain. The State Co., 1924.
   With Aesop Along the Black Border. The State Co., 1924.
   La Guerre, A Gascon of the Black Border. The State Co., 1924.

Green, Paul: *Wide Fields.* McBride, New York, 1928.
Griggs, Sutton E.: *Unfettered.* Nashville, Tenn., 1902.
   The Hindered Hand. Nashville, Tenn., 1905.
Haigh, Richmond: *An Ethiopian Saga.* Henry Holt, New York, 1919.
Harris, Joel Chandler: (See under Folklore.)
Heyward, DuBose: *Porgy.* Doran, New York, 1925.
   Mamba's Daughter. (Announced.)
Heyward, Jane Scriven: *Brown Jackets.* The State Co., Columbia, S. C., 1923.
Hobson, Anne: *In Old Alabama.* Doubleday, Page, Garden City, N. Y., 1903.
Hopkins, Pauline: *Contending Forces.*
Johnson, E. A.: *Light Ahead for the Negro.* Grafton Press, New York, 1904.
Johnson, Fenton: *Tales of Darkest Africa.* The Favorite Magazine Publishers, Chicago, 1920.
Johnson, James Weldon: *The Autobiography of an Ex-Coloured Man.* Knopf, New York, 1927.
Johnston, Mary: *The Slave Ship.* Little, Brown, Boston, 1924.
   (See *Works*)
Jones, Henry Joshua: *By Sanction of Law.*
Joseph, Gaston: *Elaine Wood* (Tr.). Danielson, London, 1923.
   Koffi. Danielson, London, 1923.
Kennedy, R. Emmet: *Black Cameos.* A. & C. Boni, New York, 1924.
   Gritney People. Dodd Mead, New York, 1928.
Kester, Paul: *His Own Country.* The Bobbs-Merrill Co., Indianapolis, 1917.
King, Grace Elizabeth: *Monsieur Motte.* Doran, New York, 1907.
   (See *Works*)
Larsen, Nella: *Quick Sands.* Knopf, New York, 1928.
Liscomb, Harry F.: *The Prince of Washington Square.* Frederick A. Stokes, New York, 1925.
Lloyd, J. U.: *Stringtown on the Pike, a Tale of Northmost Kentucky.* Dodd, Mead, New York, 1900.
MacIntyre, W. Irwin: *Colored Soldiers.* The J. W. Burke Co., Macon, Ga., 1923.
Mackenzie, J. K.: *African Clearings.* Houghton Mifflin, Boston, 1924.
Majette, Vara A.: *White Blood.* The Stratford Co., Boston, 1924.
Maran, René: *Batoula.* Seltzer, New York, 1921.
Martin, George Madden: *Children in the Mist.* Appleton, New York, 1920.
McBlair, Robert: *Mister Fish Kelly.* Appleton, New York, 1924.
McFarland, Haldane: *The Wooings of Jezebel Pettifer.* Knopf, New York, 1925.
McGirt, James E.: *The Triumph of Ephraim.* Philadelphia, 1907.
McKay, Claude: *Home to Harlem.* Harper, New York, 1928.
McLean, Eddie: *Sweet Old Days in Dixie.* Edwards and Broughton, Raleigh, N. C., 1907.

Means, E. K.: *E. K. Means.* Putnam's, New York, 1918.
   More E. K. Means. Putnam's, New York, 1919.
   Further E. K. Means. Putnam's, New York, 1921.
Merrick, Leonard: *The Quaint Companions.* E. P. Dutton, New York, 1924.
Mischeaux, Oscar: *The Conquest.* The Woodruff Press, Lincoln, Neb., 1913.
Millin, Sarah Gertrude: *Dark River.*
   God's Step-Children. Boni and Liveright, New York, 1924.
Morrow, Honoré W.: *Forever Free.* William Morrow Co., New York, 1927.
Mott, Ed.: *Black Homer of Jimtown.* Grosset, New York, 1900.
Nassau, Robert Hamill: *Where Animals Talk.* Badger, Boston, 1912.
O'Brien, Edward J.: *Best Short Stories of 1923—.* Small, Maynard, Boston, 1924—.
O. Henry Memorial Award Prize Stories of 1925—. Doubleday, Page, Garden City, N. Y., 1926—.
Ovington, Mary White: *Hazel.* The Crisis Pub. Co., N. Y., 1913.
   The Shadow. Harcourt, Brace, New York, 1920.
Page, Thomas Nelson: *In Ole Virginia; or Marse Chan and Other Stories.* Scribner, New York, 1910. (Also collected works.)
Peterkin, Julia: *Green Thursday.* Knopf, New York, 1924.
   Black April. Bobbs-Merrill Co., Indianapolis, 1927.
Phillpotts, Eden: *Black, White and Brindled,* Macmillan, New York, 1923.
Pickens, Williams: *Bursting Bonds.* Jordan and More Press.
   The Vengeance of the Gods. A. M. E. Book Concern, Philadelphia, 1922.
Powys, Llewelyn: *Ebony and Ivory.* Harcourt, Brace, New York, 1924.
   Black Laughter. Harcourt, Brace, 1924.
Pratt, Lucy: *Ezekiel Expands.* Houghton Mifflin, Boston, 1914. 1914.
   Ezekiel. Doubleday, Page, Garden City, N. Y., 1909.
Rutledge, Archibald: *Tom and I on the Old Plantation.* Stokes, New York, 1918.
Sanborn, Gertrude: *Veiled Aristocrats.* The Associated Publishers, Washington, D. C., 1924.
Scarborough, Dorothy: *In the Land of Cotton.* Macmillan, New York, 1923.
Schreiner, Olive: *From Man to Man.* Harper, New York, 1927.
Scott, Evelyn: *Migrations.* A. & C. Boni, New York, 1927.
Shackelford, Wm. H.: *Along the Highway.* Nashville, Tenn., 1915.
Shands, H. A.: *White and Black.* Harcourt, Brace, New York, 1922.
Shaw-Fullilove, Maggie: *Who Was Responsible.* The Abingdon Press, Cincinnati, Ohio, 1919.
Smith, F. H.: *Colonel Carter of Cartersville.* Houghton Mifflin, Boston, 1901. (See *Works.*)
Sparkling, E. Earl: *Under the Levee.* Scribner, New York, 1925.
Strachey, Ray (pseudonym of Mrs. Rachel Costelloe Strachey): *Marching On.* Harcourt, Brace, New York, 1923.

Stribling, T. S.: *Birthright*. The Century Co., New York, 1922.
Stuart, Mrs. Ruth McEnery: *Napoleon and Jackson*. The Century Co., New York, 1902.
  The Second Wooing of Salina Sue and Other Stories. Harper, New York and London, 1905.
  Aunt Amity's Silver Wedding and Other Stories. The Century Co., New York, 1909.
Tharaud, Jerome and Jean: *The Long Walk of Samba Diouf*. Duffield and Co., New York, 1924. (Tr. by Willis Steele.)
Tinker, Edward Larocque: *Toucoutou*. Dodd, Mead, New York, 1928.
Toomer, Jean: *Cane*. Boni and Liveright New York, 1923. (New edition, 1927.)
Tracy, R. Archer: *The Sword of Nemesis*. The Neale Publishing Co., New York, 1919.
Twain, Mark: *Pudd'nhead Wilson*. (Collected works.) Harper, New York. 1910. (See *Works*.)
Underwood, Edna Worthley: *The Penitent*. Houghton Mifflin, 1922.
Van Vechten, Carl: *Nigger Heaven*. Knopf, New York, 1926.
Vassal, William F.: *Under the Skin*. F. Stone Williams Co., Brooklyn, N. Y., 1923.
Walker, Thomas, H. B.: *J. Johnson or the Unknown Man*. The E. O. Painter Printing Co., Deland, Florida, 1915.
Walrond, Eric: *Tropic Death*. Boni and Liveright, New York, 1926.
  Big Ditch. Boni and Liveright, New York, 1928.
White, Walter: *The Fire in the Flint*. Knopf, New York, 1924.
  Flight, Knopf, 1926.
Wiley, George: *Southern Plantation Stories and Sketches*. New York, 1905.
Wiley, Hugh: *The Wildcat*. Doran, New York, 1920.
Wilson, Romer: *Latter Day Symphony*. Knopf, New York, 1927.
  Lily. Knopf, New York, 1923.
Wood, Clement: *Nigger*. Dutton, New York, 1922.
Woodson, C. G.: *African Stories*. The Association for the Study of Negro Life and History, Inc., Washington, D. C.
Wright, Zara: *Black and White Tangled Threads*. Chicago, 1920.
Wylie, I. A. R.: *Black Harvest*. Doran, New York, 1926.
Young, Frances Brett: *Woodsmoke*. Dutton, New York, 1924.
  Marching on Tanga. Dutton, New York, 1918.
  Pilgrim's Rest, Dutton, New York, 1923.
  Sea Horses. Knopf, New York, 1925.

III. Drama

Basshe, Em Jo: *Earth*. Macaulay Co., New York, 1927.
Boucicault, Dion: *The Octoroon*. (Reprinted in *Representative American Plays*, edited by A. Hobson Quinn.) Scribner, New York, 1917.

Bruce, Richard: *Sahdji*. (In *Plays of Negro Life*, edited by Alain Locke and Montgomery Gregory.) Harper, New York, 1927.
Cohen, Octavus Roy: *Come Seven*. Longmans, Green and Co., New York, 1926.
Culbertson, Ernest Howard: *Goat Alley*. Stewart, Kidd, Cincinnati, 1922.
(One-act version in *Twenty Contemporary One-Act Plays*. Appleton, New York, 1922.)
Rackey. (In *Plays of Negro Life*.)
Duncan, Thelma: *The Death Dance*. (In *Plays of Negro Life*.)
Gold, Michael: *Hoboken Blues*. (In *The American Caravan*, Macaulay Co, New York, 1927.)
Green, Paul: *The No 'Count Boy*. Holt, New York, 1925.
In Aunt Mahaly's Cabin. Samuel French, New York, 1925.
The Man Who Died at Twelve O'Clock. French, 1925.
Lonesome Road. McBride, New York, 1926.
The Field God and *In Abraham's Bosom*. McBride, 1927.
In the Valley. French, 1927.
Supper for the Dead. French, 1927.
Gregory, Montgomery: (See Locke, Alain.)
Grimke, Angelina: *Rachel*. The Cornhill Co., Boston, 1920.
Heyward, DuBose and Dorothy: *Porgy*. Doubleday, Page, New York, 1927.
Johnson, Georgia Douglas: *Plumes*. (In *Plays of Negro Life*.)
Blue Blood. (In *Fifty More Contemporary One-Act Plays*. Appleton, New York, 1928.)
Locke, Alain and Gregory, Montgomery: Editors of *Plays of Negro Life*. Harper, New York, 1927.
Martin, Mrs. George Madden: *The Lion's Mouth*. Appleton, New York, 1920.
Matheu, John: *Cruiter*. (In *Plays of Negro Life*.)
O'Neill, Eugene: *The Dreamy Kid*.
The Emperor Jones.
All God's Chillun Got Wings.
(All in *Collected Works*. Boni and Liveright, New York, 1924)
Richardson, Willis: *Compromise*. (In *The New Negro*. A. & C. Boni, New York, 1925.)
The Flight of the Natives. (In *Plays of Negro Life*.)
The Broken Banjo. (In *Plays of Negro Life*.)
The Chip Woman's Fortune. (In *Fifty More Contemporary One-Act Plays*. Appleton, New York, 1928)
Rogers, John Williams, Jr.: *Judge Lynch*. French, New York, 1924.
Spence, Eulalie: *The Starter*. (In *Plays of Negro Life*.)
The Fool's Errand. French, 1927.
Stowe, Harriet Beecher: *Uncle Tom's Cabin*. (Reprinted.) French, New York.

Toomer, Jean: *Kabnis*. (In *Cane*. Boni and Liveright, New York, 1923; republished, 1927.)
  Balo (In *Plays of Negro Life*.)
Torrence, Ridgely: *Granny Maumee, The Rider of Dreams, Simon the Cyrenian*. Macmillan, New York, 1917.
  The Danse Calinde. (In *Plays of Negro Life*.)
White, Lucy: *The Bird Child*. (In *Plays of Negro Life*.)
Wilson, Frank: *Sugar Cane*. (In *Plays of Negro Life*.)

IV. Folklore, Folksong, and Music

Abbott, F. H.: *Eight Negro Songs*. Enoch and Sons, 1924.
Ballanta, N. G. J., and Taylor, A.: *St. Helena Island Spirituals*. Schirmer, New York, 1925.
Barrett, H.: *Negro Folk Songs*. The Hampton Press, Hampton, Va., 1912.
Barton, Wm. E.: *Old Plantation Hymns*. Lawson, Wolffe and Co.
Benedict, Helen D.: *Bellair Plantation Melodies*. New Orleans, 1924.
Blackburn, Mary Johnson: *Folk Lore Mammy Days*. Boston, 1924.
Burleigh, Harry T.: *Plantation Melodies, Old and New*. (With R. S. Phillips, J. E. Campbell, and Paul Laurence Dunbar.) Schirmer, New York, 1901.
Cotten, S. S.: *Negro Folk Lore Stories*. Charlotte Federation of Women's Clubs, Charlotte, N. C., 1923.
Cronise, Florence M.: (With Ward, Henry W.) *Cunnie Rabbit, Mr. Spider and Other Beef*. London, 1903.
Cross, Tom Peete: *Witchcraft in North Carolina*. University of N. C. Press, Chapel Hill, N. C., 1920.
Culbertson, A. V.: *At the Big House Where Aunt Nancy and Aunt Phrony Held Forth on Animal Talk*. Indianapolis, 1904, 1905.
Curtis-Burlin, Natalie (The Hampton Series): *Negro Folk Songs*. (Books 1 and 2—Spirituals, Books 3 and 4—Work and Play Songs.) Schirmer, New York, 1918.
  Songs and Tales from the Dark Continent. Schirmer, New York, 1920.
Dann, Hollis (With Loomis, H. W.): *Forty-Eight Spirituals for Choral Use*. Burchard Co., Boston, 1924.
Davenport, F. M.: *Primitive Traits in Religious Revivals*. New York, 1905.
Davis, Sidney F.: *Mississippi Negro Lore*. Jackson, Tenn., 1914.
Dett, R. Nathaniel: *Religious Folk Songs of the Negro*. Schirmer, New York, 1925.
Fell, J. R.: *Folk Tales of the Batonga and Other Sayings*. Holborn Publishing House, London, 1923.
Fenner, Thomas P.: *Religious Folk Songs of the Negro*. The Institute Press, Hampton, Va. (Reprinted in 1924 from the edition of 1909.)
Fisher, William Arms (With Harvey B. Gaul, J. Rosamond Johnson, and Charles F. Manney.): *Ten Negro Spirituals*. Oliver Ditson Co., Boston, 1925.
  Seventy Negro Spirituals. Oliver Ditson Co., 1927.

BIBLIOGRAPHIES AND DIRECTORIES 87

Fitzjames, J.: *Bahaman Folk Lore*. Montreal, 1906.
Frey, Hugo (Editor): *Twenty-Five Negro Spirituals*. Robins, Engel Co., New York, 1924.
Gaul, Harvey B.: (See Fisher, W. A.)
Handy, W. C.: *Blues, an Anthology* (with an introduction by Abbe Niles). A. & C. Boni, New York, 1926.
Halowell, Emily: *Calhoun Plantation Songs*. C. W. Thompson Co., Boston. 1921.
Hare, Maud Cuney: *Six Creole Songs*. The Carl Fischer Co., New York, 1921.
Harris, Joel Chandler: *The Tar Baby*. Appleton, New York, 1904.
  On the Plantation. New York, 1905.
  Bishop and Boogerman. New York, 1909.
  Uncle Remus Returns. Houghton Mifflin, 1918.
  Uncle Remus, His Songs and His Sayings. Appleton, 1920.
Honeij, James Albert: *South African Folk Tales*. The Baker & Taylor Co., New York, 1910.
Jessye, Eva: *My Spirituals*. Robbins, Engel Co., New York, 1927.
Johnson, Guy B.: (See Odum, Howard W.)
Johnson, Guy B.: *John Henry*. (announced). U. N. C. Press, Chapel Hill.
Johnson, J. Rosamond: (See Fisher, W. A. and Johnson, James Weldon).
Johnson, James Weldon: *The Book of American Negro Spirituals*. (With J. Rosamond Johnson.) The Viking Press, New York, 1925.
  The Second Book of American Negro Spirituals. (With J. Rosamond Johnson.) The Viking Press, 1926.
Jones, Charles C., Jr.: *Negro Myths from the Georgia Coast*. The State Co., Columbia, S. C.
Kennedy, R. Emmet: *Mellows, a Chronicle of Unknown Singers*. (Negro Work Songs, Street Cries, and Spirituals.) A. & C. Boni, New York, 1925.
Krehbiel, Henry Edward: *Afro-American Folk Songs*. Schirmer, New York, 1914.
Loomis, H. W.: (See Dann, Hollis.)
Lovingood, P.: *Famous Negro Musicians*. Brooklyn Forum Press, Brooklyn, 1921.
Manney, Charles F.: (See Fisher, W. A.)
McBride, J. M.: *Brer Rabbit in the Folk Tales of the Negro and Other Races*. Sewanee, Tenn., 1911.
Metfessel, Milton: *Phonophotography in Folk Music*. University of North Carolina Press, Chapel Hill, N. C., 1928.
Music Composed by Negroes. Bulletin of Community Service. Bureau of Community Music, 315 Fourth Ave., New York City.
Niles, John J.: *Singing Soldiers*. Scribner, New York, 1927.
Odum, Howard W.: *The Negro and His Songs*. (With Guy B. Johnson.) University of North Carolina Press, Chapel Hill, N. C., 1925.
  Negro Workaday Songs. (With Guy B. Johnson.) University of North Carolina Press, 1926.

Parsons, Elsie Clews: *Folklore of the Sea Islands, South Carolina.* The American Folklore Society, New York, 1923.
Peterson, Clara G.: *Creole Songs from New Orleans,* New Orleans, 1902.
Puckett, N. N.: *Folk Beliefs of the Southern Negro.* University of North Carolina Press, Chapel Hill, N. C., 1926.
Sandburg, Carl: *The American Songbag.* Harcourt, Brace, New York, 1928.
Scarborough, Dorothy: *On the Trail of Negro Folk Songs.* Harvard University Press, Cambridge, Mass., 1925.
"Shepperd, Eli": *Plantation Songs.* R. H. Russell Publishers, New York, 1901.
Sims, Marie H.: *Negro Mystic Lore.* Chicago, 1907.
Stewart, Ruth McEnery: *Plantation Songs.* Appleton, New York, 1916.
Talley, Thomas W.: *Negro Folk Rhymes.* Macmillan, New York, 1922.
Taylor, A.: (See Ballanta, N. G. J.)
Turner, Harriet: *Folk Songs of the American Negro.* Boston Music Co., 1925.
White, Clarence Cameron: *Forty Negro Spirituals.* Presser Co., Philadelphia, 1928.
White, Newman I.: *American Negro Folk Songs.* Harvard University Press, Cambridge, Mass. 1928.
Work, F. J.: *Some American Negro Folk Songs.* Boston, 1909.
Work, John Wesley: *Folk Songs of the American Negro.* Fisk University Press, Nashville, Tenn., 1915.
Young, M.: *Plantation Bird Legends.* New York, 1902.

V. GENERAL

American Negro Academy, Publications of. Washington, D. C.
Atlanta University Studies (Edited by W. E. B. DuBois.): Atlanta, Ga., 1896-1911.
Baker, Ray Stannard: *Following the Color Line.* Doubleday, Page, 1908.
Boris, J. J. (ed.): *Who's Who in Colored America.* Who's Who in Colored America Corporation, New York, 1927.
Braithwaite, William Stanley: *The Poetic Year, a Critical Anthology.* Small, Maynard, Boston, 1916.
The Story of the Great War. Stokes, New York, 1919.
Brawley, Benjamin G.: *History of Morehouse College.* Atlanta, 1917.
The Negro in Literature and Art. Duffield, New York. 1917 (Revised edition 1921.).
Africa and the War. Duffield, New York, 1918.
Your Negro Neighbor. Macmillan, New York, 1918.
Women of Achievement. New York and Chicago, 1918, 1919.
A Short History of the American Negro. Macmillan, 1919. (Revised edition.)
A Social History of the American Negro. Macmillan, 1921.
A Short History of the English Drama. Harcourt Brace, New York, 1921.
A New Survey of English Literature. Knopf, New York, 1925.

Bullock, Ralph W.: *In Spite of Handicap.* Association Press, 1928.
Cambridge History of American Literature. Putnam's, New York, 1921.
Capehart: *Reminiscences of Isaac and Sukey, Slaves of B. F. Moore.* Edwards and Broughton, Raleigh, N. C., 1907.
Corrothers, James David: *In Spite of the Handicap,* an Autobiography. Doran, New York, 1916.
Covarrubias, Miguel: *Negro Drawings.* Knopf, New York, 1928.
Crowell, J. W.: *The Negro in American History.* American Negro Academy, Washington, D. C., 1914.
Culp, D. W.:*Twentieth Century Negro Literature.* J. L. Nichols Co., Naperville, Ill., 1902.
Detweiler, Frederick G.: *The Negro Press in the United States.* University of Chicago Press, 1923.
Dowd, Jerome: *The Negro in American Life.* The Century Co., New York, 1926.
DuBois, W. E. B.: *The Souls of Black Folk.* A. C. McClurg, Chicago, 1903.
The Negro in the South (With Booker T. Washington.). Jacobs & Co., Philadelphia, 1907.
John Brown. Jacobs & Co., Philadelphia, 1909.
The Negro. (Home University Library.) Holt, New York, 1915.
Darkwater. Harcourt, Brace, New York, 1920.
The Gift of Black Folk. The Stratford Co., Boston, 1924.
Dunbar, Alice M. Nelson: *Masterpieces of Negro Eloquence.* Bookey Publishing Co., New York, 1914.
Ellis, George W.: *Negro Culture in West Africa.* Neale Publishing Co., New York, 1914.
Fauset, Arthur Huff: *For Freedom.* Franklin Publishing Co., Philadelphia, 1927.
Frazer, W. H.: *Fireside Musings of "Uncle Rastus" and "Aunt Randy."* Murrill Co., Charlotte, N. C., 1925.
Fry, Roger: *Vision and Design.* Brentano's, New York, 1921.
Gaines, Francis Pendleton: *The Southern Plantation.* Columbia University Press, New York, 1925.
Gore, George W.: *Negro Journalism.* DePauw University, Greencastle, Ind., 1922.
Guérard, Albert: *Beyond Hatred.* Scribner, New York, 1925.
Guillaume, Paul (and Munro, Thomas.): *Primitive Negro Sculpture.* Harcourt, Brace, New York, 1926.
Hammond, Lily Hardy: *In Black and White.* Fleming H. Revell Co., New York, 1914.
Hortzclaw, W. H.: *The Black Man's Burden.* New York, 1915.
Hubbard, Elbert: *Little Journeys to the Homes of Great Teachers.* (Booker T. Washington.) Roycrofters, Aurora, N. Y., 1908.

Jackson, W. C.: (See White, Newman I.)
Johns Hopkins University: *Studies Relating to the Negro*. Baltimore, Md.
Johnson, Charles S. (Editor): *Ebony and Topaz*. Opportunity, New York, 1927.
Johnson, Julia E.: *The Negro Problem*. 1921.
Jones, Laurence C.: *Piney Woods and Its Story*. Fleming H. Revell Co., New York, 1922.
Journal of Negro History: Edited by Carter G. Woodson, Washington, D. C.
Kerlin, Robert J.: *Negro Poets and Their Poems*. Associated Publishers, Inc., Washington, D. C., 1922.
   The Voice of the Negro. Dutton, New York, 1920.
King, Willis J.: *The Negro in American Life*. Methodist Book Concern, 1926.
Library of Southern Literature. Martin and Hoyt, Atlanta, 1907.
Locke, Alain (Editor): *The New Negro*. A. & C. Boni, New York, 1925.
Lovingood, P.: *Famous Negro Musicians*. The Brooklyn Forum Press, New York, 1921.
Maran, René (Tr. by Alain Locke.): *Kongo*. A. & C. Boni, New York, 1928.
Millin, Sarah G.: *The South Africans*. Boni and Liveright, New York, 1927.
Miller, Kelly: *Race Adjustment*. Neale Publishing Co., New York, 1908.
   Out of the House of Bondage. Neale, 1914.
   Appeal to Conscience. Macmillan, New York, 1913.
Milligan, Harold Vincent: *Stephen Collins Foster*—a Biography. Schirmer, New York, 1920.
Mims, Edwin: *The Advancing South*. Doubleday, Page, Garden City, 1926.
Modern Eloquence, volume IX: George L. Shuman, Chicago, 1903.
Morton, Beatrice: *Negro Poetry in America*. The Stratford Co., Boston, 1925.
Moses, Montrose J.: *The Literature of the South*. Crowell, New York, 1910.
Mossell, Mrs. N. F.: *Afro-American Women*. Philadelphia, 1918.
Moton, R. R.: *Finding a Way Out*. New York, 1920.
Munro, Thomas: (See Guillaume, Paul).
Murray, Daniel: *Encyclopedia of the Negro*. Washington, D. C., 1912.
Negro Year Book (An Annual Encyclopedia of the Negro.). Published by the Department of Records and Research, Tuskegee Normal and Industrial Institute, Tuskegee, Ala. Edited by Monroe N. Work.
O'Brien, Edward J.: *The Advance of the American Short Story*. Dodd, Mead, New York, 1923.
Odum, Howard W.: *Rainbow Round My Shoulder*. Bobbs-Merrill Co., Indianapolis, 1928.
   Social and Mental Traits of the Negro. Longmans, Green, New York, 1910.
   (Editor) *Southern Pioneers*. U. N. C. Press, 1926.
Ovington, Mary White: *Portraits in Color*. Viking Press, New York, 1927.

Page, Thomas Nelson: *The Negro, the Southerner's Problem.* Scribner, New York, 1904.
Park, Robert Emory: (See Washington, Booker T.)
Pattee, Fred Lewis: *A History of American Literature.* The Century Co., New York, 1915.
Peabody, Francis G.: *Education for Life.* Doubleday, Page, Garden City, 1922.
Phillips, Ulrich B.: *Plantation and Frontier.* Arthur Clark Co., Cleveland, 1910.
American Negro Slavery. Appleton, New York, 1918.
Pickens, William: *The Heir of Slaves.* Neale Publishing Co., New York, 1911.
Price, Willard: *The Negro Around the World.* Doran, New York, 1925.
Pringle, Elizabeth W. A.: *Chronicle of Chicora Wood.* Scribner, New York, 1922.
Reuter, E. B.: *The American Race Problem.* Crowell, New York, 1927.
Roman, Charles Victor: *American Civilization and the Negro.* F. A. Davis Co., Philadelphia, 1916.
Rosenfeld, Paul: *Men Seen.* The Dial Press, New York, 1925.
Rowland, Mabel: *Bert Williams, Son of Laughter.* English Crafters, New York, 1923.
Royce, Josiah: *The Race Question and Other American Problems.* Macmillan, New York, 1908.
Sandburg, Carl: *The Chicago Race Riots.* Harcourt, Brace, New York, 1919.
Scarborough, Dorothy: *From a Southern Porch.* Putnam's, New York, 1911.
Schomburg, Arthur A.: *A Bibliographical Checklist of American Negro Poetry.* Charles F. Heartmann, New York, 1916.
Scott, Emmett J.: *Booker T. Washington, Builder of a Civilization.* Doubleday, Page, Garden City, N. Y., 1916.
Official History of the American Negro During the World War. Washington, D. C., 1919.
Seawell, Joseph Lacy: *Law Tales for Laymen.* Alfred Williams, Raleigh, N. C., 1925.
Seldes, Gilbert: *The Seven Lively Arts.* Harper, New York, 1924.
Seligman, H. J.: *The Negro Faces America.* Harper, New York, 1920.
Sergeant, Elizabeth Shipley: *Fire Under the Andes.* Knopf, New York, 1927.
The South in the Building of the Nation. Southern Historical Publication Society, Richmond, Virginia, 1909.
Sterling, Ada: *A Belle of the Fifties.* Doubleday, Page, Garden City, N. Y., 1905.
Stoddard, Lothrop: *The Rising Tide of Color.* Scribner, New York, 1920.
Streeter, Daniel W.: *Denatured Africa.*
Talbot, Edith Armstrong: *True Religion in Negro Hymns.* (A Reprint from *The Southern Workman.*)

Tannenbaum, Frank: *Darker Phases of the South.* Putnam's, New York, 1924.
Thrasher, Max Bennett: *Tuskegee.* Small, Maynard, Boston, 1901.
Untermeyer, Louis: *American Poetry Since 1900.* Holt, New York, 1923.
Vandercook, John W.: *Tom-Tom.* Harper, 1926.
    Black Majesty. Harper, New York, 1928.
Ward, Herbert: *A Voice From the Congo.* Scribner, New York, 1910.
Washington, Booker T.: *The Story of My Life and Work.* Nichols and Co., Naperville, Ill., 1900.
    Up From Slavery: An Autobiography. Doubleday, Page, Garden City, 1901.
    Character Building. Doubleday, Page, 1902.
    Working With the Hands. Doubleday, Page, 1904.
    Putting the Most Into Life. Crowell, New York, 1906.
    Frederick Douglass. (In *American Crisis Biographies.*). George W. Jacobs, Philadelphia, 1907.
    The Negro in the South (With W. E. B. DuBois.). George W. Jacobs, Philadelphia, 1907.
    The Negro in Business. Hertel, Jenkins and Co., Chicago, 1907.
    The Story of the Negro. Doubleday, Page, Garden City, New York, 1909.
    My Larger Education. Doubleday, Page, 1911.
    The Man Farthest Down (With Robert Emory Park.). Doubleday, Page, New York, 1912.
Weatherford, W. D.: *The Negro from Africa to America.* Doran, New York, 1924.
Whiteman, Paul: *Jazz.* J. H. Sears Co., New York, 1926.
Wiggins, Lida Keck: *The Life and Works of Paul Laurence Dunbar.* J. L. Nichols Co., Naperville, Ill., 1920.
Williams, Charles: *Sidelights on Negro Soldiers.* B. J. Brimmer, Boston, 1923.
Wilson, Peter Mitchell: *Southern Exposure.* University of N. C. Press, 1927.
Woodson, Carter G.: *The Negro in Our History.* Associated Publishers, Washington, D. C., 1922.
    Negro Orators and Their Orations. Associated Publishers, Washington, 1922.
    Free Negro Heads of Families in the United States in 1830. The Association for the Study of Negro Life and History, Washington, D. C., 1925.
    The Mind of the Negro as Reflected in Letters Written During the Crisis, 1800-1860. The Association for the Study of Negro Life and History, Washington, 1926.
Wyeth, John A.: *With Sabre and Scalpel.* Harper, New York, 1914.
Zayas, De M.: *African Negro Art: Its Influence on Modern Art.* New York, 1916.

PUBLISHERS' DIRECTORY

(Numerals refer to chapters)

Allyn & Bacon, 50 Beacon St., Boston, Mass. (9, 10)
Appleton, (D.) & Co., 35 W. 42nd St., New York, (1, 2, 5, 6, 7, 9, 10)
Associated Publishers, Washington, D. C. (1, 2, 3, 13)
Association for the Study of Negro History, Washington, D. C. (13)
Bobbs-Merrill Co., 18 University Sq., Indianapolis, Ind. (9, 10, 11)
Boni (A. & C.), 66 Fifth Ave., New York. (1, 2, 3, 4, 5, 6, 7, 9, 10, 12, 13, 14)
Boni & Liveright, 61 W. 48th St., New York. (2, 5, 7, 10, 11, 12)
Brentano's, 5th Ave. and 27th St., New York. (7)
Brimmer (B. J.) Co., 384 Boylston St., Boston, Mass. (2, 3)
Burke, (J. W.) Co., Macon, Georgia. (9)
Century Co., 353 Fourth Ave., New York. (6, 9, 10)
Columbia University Press, 2960 Broadway, New York. (1, 2, 5, 6, 9, 10)
Cornhill Publishing Co., 2 A Park St., Boston, Mass. (5)
Crisis Publishing Co., 69 Fifth Ave., New York. (10)
Crowell (Thomas Y.) Co., 393 Fourth Ave., New York. (9, 10, 13)
Dial Press, 152 W. 13th St., New York, (2, 3, 13, 14)
Dodd, Mead & Co., 443 Fourth Ave., New York. (1, 9, 10)
Doran. Now Doubleday, Doran.
Doubleday, Doran & Co., Inc., Garden City, New York. (9, 10, 11, 12, 13, 14)
Doubleday, Page. Now Doubleday, Doran.
Duffield & Co., 200 Madison Ave., New York. (1, 2, 3, 5, 6, 7, 9, 10, 13)
Duke University Press, Durham, N. C. (1, 5)
Dutton (E. P.) Co., 681 Fifth Ave., New York. (4, 6, 9, 10, 13, 14)
English Crafters, Rochester, New York. (5)
Fisk University Press, Nashville, Tenn. (1, 13, 14)
Franklin Publishing Co., Philadelphia, Penn. (13, 14)
French (Samuel), 25 W. 45th St., New York. (5, 6, 8, 9)
Harcourt, Brace & Co., 383 Madison Ave., New York. (1, 2, 3, 4, 5, 10, 13)
Harper & Bros., 49 E. 33rd St., New York, (1, 2, 3, 4, 5, 6, 7, 8, 9, 10, 12)
Harvard University Press, Randall Hall, Cambridge 38, Mass. (1, 13)
Holt (Henry) & Co., 1 Park Ave., New York. (2, 3, 4, 8, 13)
Houghton Mifflin Co., 4 Park St., Boston, Mass. (9, 10)
Jacobs (G. W.), Philadelphia, Penn. (13)
Kennerley, Mitchell, 489 Park Ave., New York. (4)
Knopf (A. A.), Inc., 730 Fifth Ave., New York. (3, 4, 5, 6, 9, 10, 11, 12)
Little, Brown & Co., 34 Beacon St., Boston, Mass. (6, 7, 10)
Luce (J. W.) & Co., 212 Summer St., Boston, Mass. (3)
Macaulay Co., 117 E. 23rd St., New York. (8, 12)
McBride (Robert M.) & Co., 7 W. 16th St., New York. (7, 8, 9, 10, 12)
McClurg (A. C.) & Co., 333 E. Ontario St., Chicago, Ill. (1, 10, 13)

Macmillan Co., 60 Fifth Avenue, New York. (1, 2, 3, 4, 6, 7, 9, 10, 13)
Martin and Hoyt, Atlanta, Georgia. (9, 10)
National Urban League, 17 Madison Ave., New York. (2, 4, 10, 11, 12, 14)
Putnam's (G. P.) Sons, 2 W. 45th St., New York. (9, 10, 13)
Schirmer (G)., 3 East 43rd St., New York. (1, 9, 13)
Scribner's (Charles) Sons, 597 Fift Ave., New York. (1, 2, 4, 7, 8, 9, 10)
Shuman (G. L.) & Co., 22 Beacon St., Boston, Mass. (13)
Simon & Schuster, 37 W. 57th St., New York. (2, 3, 4)
Small, Maynard & Co., 41 Mt. Vernon St., Boston, Mass. (12, 13)
Southern Historical Publishing Soc., Richmond, Virginia.
Southern Publishing Co., 2015 Jackson St., Dallas, Tex. (9, 10, 13)
State Co., Columbia, S. C. (9)
Stone Publishing Co., Charlotte, N. C. (1, 2)
Stratford Co., 240 Boylston St., Boston, Mass. (1, 2, 3, 5, 6, 7, 9, 10, 13)
Turner (H. T.), Metropolitan Bank Building, Washington, D. C. (3)
University of Chicago Press, 5750 Ellis Ave., Chicago, Ill. (1, 2, 5, 7, 13, 14)
University of North Carolina Press, Chapel Hill, N. C. (1, 2, 4, 5, 9, 10, 13)
Viking Press, 12 W. 40th St., New York. (1, 2, 3, 4, 5, 10, 12, 13, 14)

OUTLINES FOR INDIVIDUAL AND GROUP STUDY

1. *Constructive Ventures in Government:* By Howard W. Odum.
2. *Town Studies:* By Harold D. Meyer.
3. *Recent Tendencies in the Theatre:* By Dougald Macmillan.
4. *Planning and Furnishing a Home:* By Mary Thomas Hobbs.
5. *Studies in the History of North Carolina:* By R. D. W. Connor.
6. *Studies in Citizenship for Women:* By D. D. Carroll.
7. *Studies in the Modern English Novel:* By G. M. McKie.
8. *Present Day Literature, 1923-1924:* By Cornelia Spencer Love.
9. *The High School Society:* By Harold D. Meyer and Clara B. Cole.
10. *A Study Course in American One-Act Plays:* By Ethel Theodora Rockwell.
11. *Public Welfare and the Community:* The North Carolina Plan.
12. *Know Your Own State—North Carolina:* By S. H. Hobbs, Jr.
13. *Great Composers:* By Paul John Weaver.
14. *Good Books, 1924-1925:* By Cornelia Spencer Love.
15. *Studies in the History of Contemporary Europe:* By Chester P. Higby.
16. *The South in Contemporary Literature:* By Addison Hibbard.
17. *A Study of Shakspere:* By Russell Potter.
18. *Studies in Southern Literature:* By Addison Hibbard.
19. *Current Books, 1925-1926:* By Cornelia Spencer Love.
20. *A Study Course in International One-Act Plays:* By Ethel T. Rockwell.
21. *Studies in the Development of the Short Story:* By Louis B. Wright.
22. *A Study Course in Modern Drama:* By Elizabeth Lay Green.
23. *Pre-School Child Study Programs:* By Harold D. Meyer.
24. *Studies in American Literature:* By Addison Hibbard.
25. *Modern French Art:* By Russell Potter.
26. *Adventures in Reading, 1926-1927:* By Russell Potter.
27. *Our Heritage:* By James H. Hanford.
28. *Contemporary American Literature:* By Paul Green and Elizabeth Lay Green.
29. *Books of Travel:* By Urban T. Holmes.
30. *Parent-Teacher Handbook for North Carolina:* By Harold D. Meyer.
31. *A Short Course on American Art and Artists:* By Mrs. Rufus L. Gwynn.
32. *A Short Course in Art History:* By Mary deB. Graves.
33. *The Negro in Contemporary American Literature:* By Elizabeth Lay Green.
34. *Other Peoples' Lives: Current Books, 1927-1928:* By Cornelia Spencer Love.

Single copies, paper binding, fifty cents each.

EXTENSION BULLETINS

Vol. I, No. 7. *Attainable Standards in Municipal Programs.* Edited by Howard W. Odum. Price 60c.
Vol. I, No. 11. *The Church and Landless Men.* L. G. Wilson and Others. Free.
Vol. II, No. 4. *Town Studies.* A Program for Women's Clubs. Harold D. Meyer. Price 50c.
Vol. II, No. 10. *The Commencement Program.* Harold D. Meyer. Price 50c.
Vol. II, No. 12. *Recent Tendencies in the Theatre.* A Program for Women's Clubs. Dougald MacMillan. Price 50c.
Vol. II, No. 13. *Agricultural Graphics*: North Carolina and the United States, 1866-1922. H. R. Smedes. Price $1.00.
Vol. III, No. 2. *Minimum Essentials and English Teaching in North Carolina High Schools.* Free.
Vol. III, No. 3. *Studies in the History of North Carolina.* A Program for Women's Clubs. R. D. W. Connor. Price 50c.
Vol. III, No. 4. *Planning and Furnishing a Home.* A Program for Women's Clubs. Mary T. Hobbs. Price 50c.
Vol. III, No. 5. *Studies in Citizenship for Women.* Revised Edition. A Program for Women's Clubs. D. D. Carroll. Price 50c.
Vol. III, No. 9. *Correlating Play and Class Room Work.* Harold D. Meyer. Price 35c.
Vol. III, No. 10. *Students in the Modern English Novel.* A Program for Women's Clubs. George McKie. Price 50c.
Vol. III, No. 11. *The Rural School Lunch.* Louise H. Snell. Price 10c.
Vol. III, No. 14. *How to Know and Use the Trees.* W. C. Coker and Enid Matherly. Price $1.00.
Vol. IV, No. 5. *A Study Course in American One-Act Plays.* A Program for Women's Clubs. Ethel T. Rockwell. Price 50c.
Vol. IV, No. 7. *Port Terminals and Water Transportation.* Debate Handbook. Price 50c.
Vol. IV, No. 10. *Public Welfare and the Community.* Free.
Vol. IV, No. 11. *Know Your Own State—North Carolina.* A Program for Women's Clubs. S. H. Hobbs, Jr. Price 50c.
Vol. IV, No. 12. *Children of Old Carolina.* Historical Pageant for Children. Ethel T. Rockwell Price 50c.
Vol. IV, No. 13. *Great Composers, 1600-1900.* A Program for Music Clubs. Paul John Weaver. Price 50c.
Vol. V, No. 3. *Good Books of 1924-1925.* A Program for Women's Clubs. Cornelia S. Love. Price 50c.
Vol. V, No. 4. *College Education and Professional Opportunity.* Compiled by T. A. Whitener. Free.
Vol. V, No. 5. *Studies in the History of Contemporary Europe.* A Program for Women's Clubs. C. P. Higby. Price 50c.
Vol. V, No. 7. *What Next in North Carolina?* North Carolina Club Year Book 1924-1925. Edited by E. C. Branson. Price 50c.
Vol. V, No. 8. *The South in Contemporary Literature.* A Program for Women's Clubs. Addison Hibbard. Price 50c.
Vol. V, No. 9. *A Study of Shakspere.* A Program for Women's Clubs. Russell Potter. Price 50c.
Vol. V, No. 10. *Studies in Southern Literature.* A Program for Women's Clubs. Revised Edition. Addison Hibbard. Price 50c.
Vol. VI, No. 3. *A Study Course in International One-Act Plays.* A Program for Women's Clubs. Ethel T. Rockwell. Price 50c.
Vol. VI, No. 4. *Studies in the Development of the Short Story: English and American.* A Program for Women's Clubs. L. B. Wright. Price 50c.
Vol. VI, No. 5. *University Lecturers.* Free.
Vol. VI, No. 6. *The Curtis-Reed Bill to Establish a Federal Department of Education.* Debate Handbook. Compiled by E. R. Rankin. Price 50c.
Vol. VI, No. 8. *Adult Education and Service through University Extension.* Free.
Vol. VI, No. 9. *Studies in Modern Drama.* Revised Edition. Elizabeth L. Green. Price 50c.
Vol. VI, No. 10. *Town and Country Interdependencies.* North Carolina Club Year Book, 1925-1926. Edited by E. C. Branson. Price 75c.
Vol. VI, No. 11. *Pre-School Child Study Programs.* Harold D. Meyer. Price 50c.
Vol. VI, No. 12. *Studies in American Literature* Revised Edition. Addison Hibbard. Price 50c.
Vol. VI, No. 13. *Modern French Art.* Russell Potter. Price 50c.
Vol. VII, No. 1. *Correspondence Catalogue, 1927-1928.* Free.
Vol. VII, No. 2. *Adventures in Reading: Current Books, 1926-1927.* Russell Potter. Price 50c.
Vol. VII, No. 3. *Extension Class Announcements. 1927-1928.* Free.
Vol. VII, No. 4. *Our Heritage: A Study through Literature of the American Tradtion.* J. H. Hanford. Price 50c.
Vol. VII, No. 5. *Contemporary American Literature.* Revised Edition. Paul and Elizabeth Lay Green. Price 50c.
Vol. VII, No. 6. *The McNary-Haugen Farm Surplus Bill.* Debate Handbook. Compiled by E. R. Rankin. Price 50c.
Vol. VII, No. 7. *Books of Travel.* Urban T. Holmes Price 50c.
Vol. VII, No. 8. *Parent-Teacher Handbook.* Fourth Edition. Edited by Harold D. Meyer. Price 50c.
Vol. VII, No. 9. *Special Legal Relations of Married Women in N. C. as to Property, Contracts, and Guardianship.* Mary P. Smith. Price 50c.
Vol. VII, No. 11. *The Child and the Home.* E. R. Groves. Price 25c.
Vol. VII, No. 12. *Some Problems in Democracy in North Carolina.* North Carolina Club Year Book. 1926-1927. Price 50c.
Vol. VII, No. 13. *High School Library Standards.* Price 50c.
Vol. VII, No. 14. *The Negro in Contemporary American Literature.* Elizabeth Lay Green. Price 50c.

MONEY ORDERS, CHECKS OR STAMPS ACCEPTED
ADDRESS: UNIVERSITY EXTENSION DIVISION,
CHAPEL HILL, N. C.

www.ingramcontent.com/pod-product-compliance
Lightning Source LLC
Chambersburg PA
CBHW031714230426

43668CB00006B/207